A gift for:

.

....

From:

....

BILLY GRAHAM

OUR GOD
of
COMFORT
and
HOPE

THOMAS NELSON
Since 1798

NASHVILLE   MEXICO CITY   RIO DE JANEIRO

Published in Nashville, Tennessee, by Thomas Nelson. Thomas Nelson is a registered trademark of HarperCollins Christian Publishing, Inc.

The contents of this book are taken from *A Treasury of Faith* by Billy Graham (Thomas Nelson, 2002) and *God's Love for You* by Billy Graham (Thomas Nelson, 2007, 2013).

Thomas Nelson titles may be purchased in bulk for educational, business, fund-raising, or sales promotional use. For information, please e-mail SpecialMarkets@ThomasNelson.com.

Unless otherwise indicated, all Scripture quotations in this book are from THE NEW KING JAMES VERSION © 1982 Thomas Nelson, Inc. Used by permission. All rights reserved.

Scripture quotations marked NIV are taken from the Holy Bible, New International Version®, NIV®. Copyright © 1973, 1978, 1984, 2011 by Biblica, Inc.™ Used by permission of Zondervan. All rights reserved worldwide. www.zondervan.com

Scripture quotations marked NRSV are taken from NEW REVISED STANDARD VERSION of the Bible. © 1989 by the Division of Christian Education of the National Council of the Churches of Christ in the U.S.A. All rights reserved.

Scripture quotations marked KJV are taken from the King James Version of the Bible.

ISBN-13: 978-0-7180-3780-2

Printed in the United States of America

15 16 17 18 19 RRD 6 5 4 3 2 1

Contents

FOREWORD

The more I read the Bible, the more I realize that love is God's supreme attribute. Behind every dealing God has with us is His perfect love. It was love that made Him create us, and it was love that caused Him to send His Son to redeem us. His love pursues us and draws us to Himself, and His love will someday take His children into His presence forever.

As with other aspects of His nature, we have a difficult time fully understanding God's love. For one thing, the word "love" has come to mean almost anything today. We say we "love" ice cream or the color of a car, or we say we "love" an entertainer or celebrity (although we've never met them and never will). But God's love is far deeper than this. His love is not a passing fancy or superficial emotion; it is a profound and unshakable commitment that seeks what is best for us. Human love may change or fade; God's love never will. He says to us, "I have loved you with an everlasting love; I have drawn you with unfailing kindness" (Jeremiah 31:3 NIV).

Don't sentimentalize God's love, however. God's love isn't a warm, fuzzy feeling that ignores sin or shuns judgment. God's holiness demands that sin be punished—but God's love has provided the way of redemption through Christ. If it weren't for God's love, we would have no hope, either in this life or the life to come.

But there is hope, because He loves us! In the following pages, I invite you to join me in discovering God's profound and abundant love for you.

Billy Graham

COMPLETE *in* GOD'S LOVE

In this is love, not that we loved God, but that He loved us.

1 JOHN 4:10

GOD'S GREATNESS

You are great, and do wondrous things;
You alone are God.

PSALM 86:10

Sometimes when I was a boy my father would drive us from our home near Charlotte to the Blue Ridge Mountains. I remember seeing them through the haze in the distance, and when they first appeared, they seemed so small, while we seemed so big in our automobile. But as we got closer to the mountains, they became huge, and we became small.

The same is true with God. Sometimes we think God must be just like we are, only a little bit bigger. But that isn't an accurate picture. He is God—and we are human. God reminded the ancient Israelites, "I am God, and not a man—the Holy One among you" (Hosea 11:9 NIV). Only when we understand His greatness will we understand our smallness.

Joyous Optimism

My soul shall be joyful in the Lord.

PSALM 35:9

When Jesus Christ is the source of our joy, no words can describe it. It is a joy "inexpressible and glorious" (1 Peter 1:8 NIV). Christ is the answer to the sadness and discouragement, the discord and division in our world. He can take discouragement and despondence out of our lives and replace them with optimism and hope.

If our hearts have been attuned to God through an abiding faith in Christ, the result will be joyous optimism and good cheer. The reason? Because we know He loves us, and nothing "shall be able to separate us from the love of God which is in Christ Jesus our Lord" (Romans 8:39).

When our confidence is in Him, discouragement gets crowded out. May that be true in your life today!

God Journeys with Us

"Lo, I am with you always, even to the end of the age."

MATTHEW 28:20

God could have created us—and then abandoned us and forgotten all about us. Many people, in fact, believe this is exactly what God must have done, or at least they act as if He did. They assume God isn't interested in them—so why should they be interested in Him? To them God is distant, remote, unconcerned about the problems and decisions they face every day.

But this isn't true! God not only put us on this journey called life, but He also wants to join us on it, if we will only let Him. We don't need to be alone, for He is with us! The Psalmist asked, "Where can I go from your Spirit? Where can I flee from your presence? If I go up to the heavens, you are there; if I make my bed in the depths, you are there" (Psalm 139:7–8 NIV).

If we understand this truth, it gives us hope—hope that our lives can be different, because God cares about us and wants to help us. No matter what happens, God will never abandon us if our trust is in Him.

Boundless Blessings

He gathers the lambs in his arms and carries them close to his heart.

Isaiah 40:11 NIV

The Old Testament gives a wonderful picture of God as our Shepherd. One psalm begins, "Hear us, o Shepherd of Israel, you who lead Joseph like a flock" (Psalm 80:1 NIV). The almighty Creator of the universe stoops to be the Shepherd of His people! A shepherd protects and feeds his sheep, and pursues them when they stray. At evening he brings them into the fold, secure against every enemy. Without the shepherd, the sheep would scatter and wander into danger.

In the best-known of all the Psalms, David makes the relationship personal. "The LORD is my shepherd," he cries exultantly, "I lack nothing." He then tells of God's constant care, until that day when "I will dwell in the house of the LORD forever" (Psalm 23:16 NIV). But the New Testament tells of another Shepherd—the Lord Jesus Christ: "I am the good shepherd. The good shepherd gives His life for the sheep" (John 10:11). He guides and protects us, and even gave His life so we will be safely in His fold forever.

The Spirit of God

I will pray the Father, and He will give you another
Helper, that He may abide with you forever.

JOHN 14:16

During His lifetime on earth, Christ's presence could be experienced only by a small group of people at any given time. Now Christ dwells through the Spirit in the hearts of all who have received Him as Savior and Lord. The Apostle Paul wrote, "Do you not know . . . that the Spirit of God dwells in you?" (1 Corinthians 3:16). The Holy Spirit is given to every believer—not for a limited time, but forever. If He left us for one moment, we would be in deep trouble.

But He doesn't! He is there to give you both the gifts and the power to work for Christ. He is there to give you strength in the moment of temptation. He is there to produce the fruit of "love, joy, peace, longsuffering, kindness, goodness, faithfulness, gentleness, self-control" (Galatians 5:22–23).

You will never have more of the Holy Spirit than you do right now.

But will He have more of you?

FRIENDS WITH GOD

There is a friend who sticks closer than a brother.

PROVERBS 18:24

Think of it: the infinite, all-powerful, holy God of the universe wants to be your friend! This is a staggering truth. He wants you to know Him personally and to discover what it means to walk with Him every day. He wants you to know He is with you, and He wants to have communication with you through His Word and through prayer. He wants to comfort you when you are upset or anxious and to encourage you when you are dejected or depressed. He wants to guide you when you face difficult decisions, and He even wants to correct you when you are about to do something foolish or wrong.

Human friends may fail us, but God never will. He wants to be our friend and for us to be His friends as well. Once you understand this, your life will never be the same.

"Come Home."

Our citizenship is in heaven, from which we also eagerly wait for the Savior.

Philippians 3:20

Once there was a widow and her son who lived in a miserable attic. Years before, she had married against her parents' wishes and had gone with her husband to live in a foreign land. He had proved irresponsible and unfaithful, and after a few years, he died without having made any provision for her and the child. It was with the utmost difficulty that she managed to scrape together the bare necessities of life.

One day the postman knocked at the attic door. The mother recognized the handwriting on the letter he brought and with trembling fingers broke the seal. There was a check and a slip of paper with just two words: "Come home." Someday a similar experience will be ours—an experience shared by all who know Christ. We do not know when the call will come. It may be when we are in the midst of our work. It may be after weeks or months of illness.

But someday a loving hand will be laid upon our shoulder and this brief message will be given: "Come home."

THE HOLINESS OF GOD

Your Redeemer is the Holy One of Israel;
He is called the God of the whole earth.

ISAIAH 54:5

We are weak and imperfect, and we can scarcely grasp the overwhelming perfection and holiness of God. We have become so used to sin that we can't imagine anyone being absolutely perfect. But God is! The Bible says, "God is light; in him there is no darkness at all" (1 John 1:5 NIV). Because God is holy, He never does wrong—never. Occasionally we hear of someone who is exceptionally good and self-sacrificing—but even then, we know they aren't perfect. Only God is perfect and holy.

From one end of the Bible to the other, God reveals Himself as absolutely pure, without flaw or blemish of any kind. When Isaiah glimpsed a vision of God, he was overwhelmed by God's holiness—and his own sinfulness. He saw angels surrounding God's throne "calling to one another: 'Holy, holy, holy is the LORD Almighty; the whole earth is full of his glory'" (Isaiah 6:3 NIV).

Only when we understand the holiness of God will we understand the depth of our sin.

PATIENCE AND PRAYER

We . . . do not cease to pray for you.

COLOSSIANS 1:9

Some years ago, a woman wrote me that she had pleaded for ten years for the conversion of her husband, but that he was more hardened than ever. I advised her to continue to plead. Sometime later I heard from her again. She said her husband was gloriously and miraculously converted in the eleventh year of her prayer vigil. How thankful she was that she had kept on praying!

The Scripture says, "Pray without ceasing" (1 Thessalonians 5:17). This should be the motto of every true follower of Jesus Christ.

Never stop praying, no matter how dark and hopeless your case may seem. Your responsibility isn't to tell God when He must act or even how He must act. Your responsibility is simply to "pray without ceasing," trusting Him to act according to His perfect will.

Only God Can Satisfy

The peace of God, which surpasses all understanding,
will guard your hearts and minds through Christ Jesus.

PHILIPPIANS 4:7

Why are we so restless? Why are we constantly searching for lasting peace and contentment, and yet never fully satisfied? "My friends all say I have everything anyone could ever want," one man wrote me recently, "but down inside I'm empty and restless. What's wrong with me?" Countless people could echo his cry, if they were honest.

The Bible says this happens to us for a very good reason: we are incomplete without God. If we leave Him out of our lives, we have an empty place in our souls, a yearning deep inside us that only God can satisfy. No matter how hard we try, if we ignore God, that hollow place stays with us, and our search for lasting peace and happiness will be futile.

Centuries ago St. Augustine wrote, "You have made us for Yourself, O God, and our hearts are restless until they find their rest in You." Only God can satisfy the deepest longings of your heart.

In the Presence of Christ

The upright shall dwell in your presence.

PSALM 140:13

What would you do if you were about to meet the Queen of England? I'm sure you would go out of your way to dress correctly and to be properly briefed so you didn't say the wrong thing or act in an improper way.

Someday you and I will meet a far greater Sovereign: the King of the universe. His dazzling glory far exceeds that of any earthly monarch, and in His presence we can only bow in humble worship and praise. Our cry will be that of Revelation: "You are worthy, O Lord, to receive glory and honor and power" (Revelation 4:11).

Are you prepared for that day when you will meet the King of kings face-to-face? No one knows the day or the hour when life will end. The time for you to prepare is now, by committing your life to Christ and beginning to live as a child of the King.

KNOWING GOD

"You shall love the LORD your God with all your heart, with all your soul, and with all your mind."

MATTHEW 22:37

Most speculations about God miss one very important truth: God wants us to know what He is like. We don't need to guess, because God has revealed Himself to us.

Suppose you decided you didn't want anyone to know you existed. What would you have to do? Not only would you have to avoid any contact with other people, but you'd also have to be sure you didn't leave any evidence around that you existed. You couldn't even put out your trash or turn on a light! Just the smallest trace would indicate you existed—and the more clues you left behind, the more convinced people would be that you were real.

This is somewhat the way it is with God. We know He exists because He has left clues behind for us to discover. But there is a crucial difference: God isn't trying to hide from us. Quite the opposite: God wants us to know He exists. Not only that, but He also wants us to know what He is like. In other words, He wants to communicate with us!

Beyond the Starry Sky

We are looking for the city that is to come.

HEBREWS 13:14 NRSV

Paul looked forward to death with great anticipation. He said, "For to me, to live is Christ, and to die is gain" (Philippians 1:21). Death for him was not an enemy to be feared, but a reality to be welcomed, in God's time. For him death was the joyous gateway to new life—the life of Heaven. Without the resurrection of Christ there could be no hope for the future. The Bible promises that someday we are going to stand face-to-face with the resurrected Christ. All our questions will be answered, and all our sorrows and fears will vanish. An old gospel hymn puts it well:

> *Face-to-face with Christ, my Savior, face-to-face—what will it be,*
> *When with rapture I behold Him, Jesus Christ who died for me?*
> *Face-to-face I shall behold Him, far beyond the starry sky;*
> *Face-to-face in all His glory, I shall see Him by and by!*

—CARRIE E. BRECK

GOD'S FOOTPRINTS

I will meditate on the glorious splendor of Your majesty,
And on Your wondrous works.

PSALM 145:5

No matter where we look, we see God's footprints.

Look up on a starry night—and you will see the majesty and power of an infinite Creator. Recently I saw a report about some recent discoveries in astronomy. It reported that astronomers now believe there may be as many as 140 billion galaxies in the known universe, some over eleven billion light years away—and each containing at least several hundred billion stars. We can't begin to imagine such distances or quantities.

God's "footprints" are everywhere, if we will but see them.

We Can Count on Him

Blessed is the man whose strength is in You.

PSALM 84:5

Someone has written a little verse that goes:

"Said the robin to the sparrow,
'I should really like to know,
Why these anxious human beings,
rush about and worry so.'
Said the sparrow to the robin,
'Friend, I think that it must be,
That they have no heavenly Father
such as cares for you and me.'"

Jesus used the carefree attitude of the birds to underscore the fact that worrying is unnatural. "Look at the birds of the air, for they neither sow nor reap . . . yet your heavenly Father feeds them" (Matthew 6:26). If He cares for tiny birds and frail flowers, why can't we count on Him for every aspect of our lives? After all, He loves us so much that He sent His Son into the world to save us. We are that valuable to Him!

In Tune with the Master

You shall surround me with songs of deliverance.

PSALM 32:7

Out West an old sheepherder had a violin, but it was out of tune. He had no way of tuning it, so in desperation he wrote to one of the radio stations and asked them at a certain hour on a certain day to strike the tone "A." The officials of the station decided they would accommodate the old fellow, and on that particular day the true tone of "A" was broadcast. His fiddle was thus tuned, and once more his cabin echoed with joyful music.

When we live apart from God, our lives get out of tune—out of harmony with others and with God. But if we live in tune with the Master, we, too, will find ourselves surrounded by His beautiful music.

Ask God to help you tune your life every day to His Word, so you can bring harmony and joy to those around you.

CHRIST IS KING

Your kingdom is an everlasting kingdom.

PSALM 145:13

The government in God's kingdom is unique. It is not a democracy where the people govern, but a "Christocracy" where Christ is the supreme authority. In a society of unredeemed people, democracy is the only fair and equitable system. But no democracy can ever be better than the people who make it up. When citizens are selfishly motivated, the government will be inequitable. When people are dishonest, the government will be the same. When everyone wants his own way, someone is going to get hurt.

But in God's kingdom, Christ is King. He is compassionate, fair, merciful, and just. When He is sovereign in men's hearts, anguish turns to peace, hatred is transformed into love, and misunderstanding into harmony. Is Christ the King of your motives and your attitudes?

A Prepared Place

In my Father's house are many mansions.

John 14:2

As much as our homes mean to us, they are not permanent. Sometimes I look at my own adult children and can hardly believe they are all grown and on their own. The house that once rang with the laughter of children now seems empty. Those disciples who for Christ's sake gave up houses and lands and loved ones knew little of home life or home joys. It was as if Jesus were saying to them, "We have no lasting home here on earth, but my Father's house is a home where we will be together for all eternity."

The venerable Bishop Ryle is reputed to have said, "Heaven is a prepared place for a prepared people, and those who enter shall find that they are neither unknown nor unexpected."

Even life's happiest experiences last but a moment, yet Heaven's joy is eternal. Someday we will go to our eternal Home—and Christ will be there to welcome us!

Rest for the Weary

"Come to Me . . . and I will give you rest."

We forget that Jesus was human as well as divine. He had calluses on His hands. If the chisel slipped and cut His finger, His blood was red and warm like ours. He knew what it meant to work long hours, to come in at night tired and weary. That is one of the reasons Jesus could say with such appeal, "Come to Me, all you who labor and are heavy laden, and I will give you rest" (Matthew 11:28).

When we are exhausted and hurting, we can take comfort from the fact that Jesus knows what it is to be exhausted and hurting also. But the greatest work Jesus did was not in the carpenter's shop, or at the marriage feast in Cana where He turned the water into wine. The greatest work Jesus did was not when He made the blind to see, the deaf to hear, the dumb to speak, or even the dead to rise.

What was His greatest work? His greatest work was what He accomplished through the Cross and Resurrection. There the burden of our sins was placed on Him, and there He won our salvation. And that is why we can come by faith to Him, and He will give us rest.

THE MESSAGE OF EASTER

"He has risen! He is not here."

MARK 16:6 NIV

The message of Easter is the central focus of Christianity. The Apostle Paul said, "If Christ has not been raised, your faith is futile; you are still in your sins" (1 Corinthians 15:17 NIV). It is as simple as that. If Christ is still dead, then He cannot be our Savior, for He was not the Son of God, and He died like all men. More than that, Heaven's doors are still locked.

But if Christ is risen, as the Scriptures teach and as hundreds of witnesses testified (none of whom ever recanted that testimony despite threats and death for many of them), then we have the ultimate hope of humanity—eternal life with the God who made us and the certainty of life beyond the grave.

What does Easter mean to you? It should mean everything, because Christ has conquered death! And that makes all the difference—now and forever!

FULL SURRENDER

"Whoever loses his life for My sake . . . will save it."

MARK 8:35

A police sergeant once asked me the secret of victorious Christian living. I told him there is no magic formula. But if any one word could describe it, it would be surrender. You may ask, "How can I surrender my life?" It is surrendered in the same way that salvation comes to the sinner. There needs to be confession of sin and a complete yielding of every area of our lives, personalities, and wills to Jesus Christ—plus faith that Christ will accept that commitment.

It's not enough for us to be confirmed or to make a decision for Christ at an altar. We cannot walk successfully in the glow of that experience for the rest of our lives. We need to return and renew those vows and covenants with the Lord. We need to take inventory and have regular spiritual checkups.

Jesus said, "If anyone desires to come after Me, let him deny himself, and take up his cross daily, and follow Me" (Luke 9:23).

Daily surrender—that's the key to daily victory.

Yielded to God

*Know ye not, that to whom ye yield yourselves servants
to obey, his servants ye are?*

ROMANS 6:16 KJV

Of Eric Liddell, the missionary and great runner whose
story is told in the film *Chariots of Fire,* someone has said,
he was "ridiculously humble in victory, utterly generous
in defeat." That's a good definition of what it means to be
meek. Eric Liddell was fiercely competitive, determined
to use his God-given abilities to the fullest. But his meekness, kindness, and gentle spirit won the admiration even
of those he defeated.

Meekness involves being yielded. The word *yield* has
two meanings. The first is negative, and the second is
positive. On one hand it means "to relinquish, to abandon." On the other hand, it also means "to give." This is
in line with Jesus' words: "He who loses [or abandons] his
life . . . will find it" (Matthew 10:39).

Those who submit to the will of God do not fight back
at life. They learn the secret of yielding—of relinquish-
ing and abandoning—their own lives and wills to Christ.
And then He gives back to them a life that is far richer and
fuller than anything they could ever have imagined.

CREATED *by* GOD'S LOVE

God is love, and he who
abides in love abides in
God, and God in him.

1 JOHN 4:16

Because of His Love

Have we not all one Father?
Has not one God created us?

MALACHI 2:10

God made us because of His love. On a human level we know that love needs an outlet—that is, it yearns to be expressed and shared. In a far greater way, God's love had to have an outlet—it had to be expressed, and it had to be shared. That is why God created Adam and Eve. And He created them in His image so they would have the ability to love also—to love each other, and to love Him. God is love—and now this wondrous characteristic of His personality was being given to Adam and Eve. What a gift! God created Adam and Eve out of love, and gave them the ability to love Him (and each other) in return.

God didn't make Adam and Eve because He was lonely, or because He needed someone to love Him in return. This is true with human love, but it isn't true with God. God is complete in Himself, and He lacks nothing. Just as an artist has a compelling urge to create a beautiful painting, so our loving God had a compelling urge to create humanity. His love was expressed in the creation of the human race.

THE RESURRECTION AND LIFE

The one who believes in me will live . . . and . . . will never die.

JOHN 11:25–26 NIV

We have three great enemies: sin, Satan, and death. Because Christ rose from the dead, we know that sin and death and Satan have been decisively defeated. And because Christ rose from the dead, we know there is life after death, and that if we belong to Him we need not fear death or hell.

Jesus said, "I am the resurrection and the life. The one who believes in me will live, even though they die; and whoever lives by believing in me will never die" (John 11:25–26 NIV). He also promised, "If I go and prepare a place for you, I will come back and take you to be with me that you also may be where I am" (John 14:3 NIV).

How hopeless our lives would be if these words were not true. Every cemetery and every grave site would be a mute witness to the futility and despair of human life. But His words are true! By God's power Jesus rose from the dead and hundreds became witnesses to His resurrection (see 1 Corinthians 15:1–8). What a glorious hope we have because Jesus is alive!

A Home in Heaven

You yourselves had [in heaven] better and lasting possessions.

HEBREWS 10:34 NIV

Paul once wrote, "If only for this life we have hope in Christ, we are of all people most to be pitied" (1 Corinthians 15:19 NIV). If there is no life after death, no Heaven, no promise of a better world, then life is empty, hopeless, without meaning or purpose. But this life is not all! Ahead is Heaven, and someday "we shall always be with the Lord" (1 Thessalonians 4:17). Someday we will go to a home where all is happiness, joy, and peace. How barren our lives would be if we didn't have this hope.

Knowing Heaven is real will make a difference in the way we live. For one thing, we won't become attached to the things of this world. We will say with Paul, "I have learned in whatever state I am, to be content" (Philippians 4:11). But Heaven should also give us a burden for those who do not have this hope. Every day you meet people who do not know Christ. Will you tell them?

CHRIST IS RISEN

"He is not here, but is risen!"

LUKE 24:6

Easter Sunday is the most triumphant and joyous day in the calendar of the Christian Church—and it should be! For many people the resurrection of Jesus Christ is symbolized by new Easter clothes or the bright color of daffodils and beautiful, white Easter lilies. But most of all, the wonder of His resurrection is symbolized in the hope that beats in the hearts of believers everywhere as they sing triumphantly: "Christ the Lord is risen today."

It is the message "Jesus is alive!" that lifts Christianity out of the category of dead superstitions and archaic religions and makes it the abiding faith of millions. The angel's message is true: "He is not here, but is risen!" And now God's promise is for you: "If you confess with your mouth the Lord Jesus and believe in your heart that God has raised Him from the dead, you will be saved" (Romans 10:9).

God Chose to Give You Life

Your hands have made me and fashioned me;
Give me understanding, that I may learn Your commandments.

Psalm 119:73

You aren't here by chance or by accident; you are here because God put you here. Long before the world was created, God knew all about you, and He planned to give you life. From all eternity you were part of His plan. No, you didn't have any choice about whether or not you would be born—but God had a choice about it, and He chose to give you life. He is the Creator of everything—including you. This journey is yours to travel—but God gave it to you. Never forget: God put you on the journey of life. We came from Him—and our greatest joy will come from giving ourselves back to Him, and learning to walk with Him every day until we return to Him.

He Suffered for You

His visage was marred more than any man.

ISAIAH 52:14

When Jesus Christ was on the Cross, His blood draining the life from His body, He knew what it was like to be alone and wracked with pain. But Jesus' pain was far more than just physical pain, for He was suffering God's judgment on all the sins of the ages—the greatest darkness of the soul ever known. As the divine Son of God, He was perfect and without sin. But all our sins were placed on Him, and He took the judgment and Hell we alone deserve. He died in our place.

Why did Jesus suffer? For you. For me. That we might have eternal life and have His peace in the midst of life's storms. That we might know that He understands our pain and suffering and stands ready to help.

Why did Jesus suffer? Because God loves us. Because God loves you, and Christ willingly went to the Cross for you. There was no other way for sin's penalty to be paid, and for us to be redeemed. The Cross is the measure of God's love. How will you respond to His love, poured out on the Cross for you?

Spiritually Nourished

"I have come that they may have life, and that they may have it more abundantly."

John 10:10

Many people go through life without ever realizing who they really are, or why God put them here. On the outside they may be successful, well-liked, even envied by others. But down inside something is still missing.

Advertisers promise happiness and fulfillment—if we will only use their product. Pundits and politicians promise abundance and world peace—if we will only listen to their wisdom or vote for them. These promises, however, always fall short. We spend all our time and energy pampering our bodies and minds—but if we ignore our souls, we will end up spiritually starved and malnourished. Don't let this happen to you!

THE PRIVILEGE OF PRAYER

"Ask, and you will receive, that your joy may be full."

JOHN 16:24

What a privilege is ours: the privilege of prayer! Just think of it—you and I have the incredible privilege of approaching the God of the Universe, "the High and Lofty One who inhabits eternity, whose name is Holy" (Isaiah 57:15)! We can only do this because Jesus Christ has opened the way.

We are to pray in times of adversity, lest we become faithless and unbelieving. We are to pray in times of prosperity, lest we become boastful and proud. We are to pray in times of danger, lest we become fearful and doubting. We are to pray in times of security, lest we become self-sufficient. Pray, believing in the promise of God's Word that "if we ask anything according to His will, He hears us" (1 John 5:14).

The Victorious Chime

I, even I, am the LORD, and besides Me there is no savior.

ISAIAH 43:11

It is said that during Napoleon's Austrian campaign his army advanced to within six miles of the town of Feldkirch. It looked as though his men would take it without resistance. But as Napoleon's army advanced toward their objective in the night, the Christians of Feldkirch gathered in their little church to pray. It was Easter eve.

The next morning at sunrise the bells of the village pealed out across the countryside. Napoleon's army, not realizing it was Easter Sunday, thought that in the night the Austrian army had moved into Feldkirch and the bells were ringing in jubilation. Napoleon ordered a retreat, and the battle at Feldkirch never took place. The Easter bells caused the enemy to flee, and peace reigned in the Austrian countryside.

As Easter is celebrated each year, churches and cathedrals around the world will ring their bells—not to sound Christ's death knell but to declare Christ's victory over death. He is the risen Lord, and because of Him our final enemy—death—has been defeated and peace reigns in our hearts!

Put Here by God

The LORD will perfect that which concerns me.

PSALM 138:8

God created us to be His friends. This was the divine plan right from the beginning, when Adam and Eve were first created—and it had its origin in the love of God.

It was, however, a friendship with a difference. On a human level we usually choose friends who are similar to us—those with like interests or a kindred personality. But God and Adam were not equals. God was the Creator; Adam was the creature. God was limitless; Adam was limited. God was independent; Adam was dependent. But in spite of the vast difference between them, God still wanted Adam and Eve to be His friends.

God's plan for Adam and Eve is also true for us. God has not changed—and neither has His purpose. We are not here by accident; we are here because God put us here—and He put us here so we could be His friends forever. Think of it: God wants you to be His friend!

THE KING OF KINGS

A scepter of righteousness is the scepter of Your kingdom.

PSALM 45:6

From His very birth, Christ was recognized as King. Something about Him inspired allegiance, loyalty, and homage. Wise men brought Him gifts. Shepherds fell down and worshiped Him. Herod, realizing that there is never room for two thrones in one kingdom, sought His life. As Jesus began His ministry, His claims upon people's lives were total and absolute. He allowed no divided loyalty. He demanded and received complete adoration and devotion. Mature men and women left their businesses and gave themselves in complete obedience to Him. Many of them gave their lives, pouring out the last full measure of devotion.

His words caused even His most avowed enemies to say, "No man ever spoke like this Man!" (John 7:46). And yet He was more than a poet, more than a statesman, more than a physician. We cannot understand Christ until we understand that He was the King of kings and the Lord of lords. Like Thomas, our only response must be to bow down and confess, "My Lord and my God!" (John 20:28).

The Great Designer

*For those who live according to the flesh set their minds on the
things of the flesh, but those who live according to the Spirit, the
things of the Spirit.*

ROMANS 8:5

God deliberately created Adam and Eve to be His friends
forever. Their fellowship with God was an unbroken reality every moment of the day.

You see, Adam and Eve weren't simply physical creatures,
they were also spiritual beings, created with a soul or spirit
that gave them the ability to know and experience God. In
fact, the Bible says they were made in God's image—that is,
God implanted something of Himself inside of them: "God
created mankind in his own image, in the image of God he
created them; male and female he created them" (Genesis
1:27 NIV). God gave them a unique spiritual nature. This
was the Great Design of the Great Designer.

This is also true of us. Like Adam and Eve, we not only
have a body and a mind, but we also have what the Bible
calls a spirit or a soul. Our souls set us apart from every
other living creature, and that makes us unique. It also
makes us fully human. Because of this, we can experience
God and have fellowship with Him.

LOVE DEMONSTRATED

He loved us and sent His Son to be the propitiation for our sins.

1 JOHN 4:10

The word *love* is used to mean many different things. We say that we "love" the house that we have just bought or that we "love" a particular vacation spot or that we "love" a peanut butter and jelly sandwich. We also "love" a certain television program, and we "love" our husband or wife. Hopefully we don't love our spouse the same way we love a peanut butter and jelly sandwich!

The greatest love of all, however, is God's love for us—a love that showed itself in action. A friend once observed, "Love talked about is easily ignored, but love demonstrated is irresistible." The Bible says "God demonstrates His own love toward us, in that while we were still sinners, Christ died for us" (Romans 5:8). Now that is real love! How will you respond to His love today?

A FRIEND OF GOD

If anyone is in Christ, he is a new creation; old things
have passed away; behold, all things have become new.

2 CORINTHIANS 5:17

Some years ago my wife and I were invited to have lunch with one of the wealthiest men in the world. He was seventy-five years old, and as he sat at the dining table, tears came down his cheeks. "I am the most miserable man in the world," he said. "I have everything anyone could ever want. If I want to go anywhere, I have my own yacht or private plane. If I want something, I can buy it, no matter what it costs. But down inside I'm miserable and empty."

Shortly after visiting that man, Ruth and I met another man who preached in a small church nearby. He was vivacious and full of life, and he told us, "I don't have a penny to my name, but I'm the happiest man in the world!" The empty space in his soul had been filled. He had become a friend of God—and that made all the difference.

COME BOLDLY

"Ask, and it will be given to you; seek, and you will find."

MATTHEW 7:7

Children are not bashful about asking for things. They would not be normal if they did not boldly make their needs known. God has said to His children, "Let us . . . come boldly to the throne of grace, that we may obtain mercy and find grace to help in time of need" (Hebrews 4:16). God is keenly aware that we are dependent upon Him for life's necessities. It was for that reason that Jesus said, "Ask, and it will be given to you; seek, and you will find; knock, and it will be opened to you" (Matthew 7:7).

What is troubling you today? Is your heart burdened because of some problem that threatens to overcome you? Are you filled with anxiety and worry, wondering what will happen next? Listen—as a child of God through faith in Christ, you can turn these over to Christ, knowing that He loves you and is able to help you. Don't carry your burden any longer, but bring it "boldly to the throne of grace"—and leave it there.

Filled with Purpose

You, O Lord, are a shield for me,
My glory and the One who lifts up my head.

Psalm 3:3

Perhaps you see your life's journey as a series of unrelated events—some good, some bad—strung together like beads on a string. Or perhaps you feel trapped like a leaf in a rushing stream, tossed about by circumstances beyond your control. Or like many people you may never have stopped to think about the road you are traveling—never asking where you came from, or why you are here, or where you are going.

But God didn't intend for our journey through life to be this way. Instead, He meant for it to be filled with joy and purpose, with even the most ordinary events being part of His plan. He also wants to guide us as we make decisions and give us hope for the future.

Blueprint for Living

I will instruct you and teach you in the way you should go;
I will guide you with My eye.

Psalm 32:8

An architect draws the plans for a new building—but it still has to be built. A composer writes a new piece of music—but it still has to be played. A chef devises a new recipe—but the ingredients still have to be cooked.

In the same way, God has given us a blueprint for living—but we must know what it is, and then put it into action. And this can happen, because God doesn't leave us to do it alone. He wants to be with us every step of the way, guiding and helping us (and even correcting us when necessary), because He loves us and wants what is best for us.

Make it your goal to seek His blueprint for your life—and then to follow it.

A God-Given Purpose

*Do not be conformed to this world, but be transformed
by the renewing of your mind.*

ROMANS 12:2

Some people are focused, using all their energies to reach
their goals. Others drift through life with little purpose or
direction, living for the moment and never thinking about
where they are headed. Most people probably live some-
where in between. But they all have this in common: they
are living only for themselves and their own happiness.

But when we come to Christ, God gives us a new
purpose. Now we want to live for Christ and not just ourselves. We begin to see other people differently—not for
what they can do for us, but what we can do for them.

When I came to Christ I had little inkling of what I
might do with my life, but down inside I knew something
was different. Before my conversion, for example, I tended
to be touchy and irritable. Now I deliberately tried to be
considerate and courteous. Little by little I was beginning
to have a new purpose in life: a desire to live for Christ. I
was learning that "those who live should no longer live for
themselves but for him who died for them and was raised
again" (2 Corinthians 5:15 NIV).

The Right Path

Teach me Your way, O Lord,
And lead me in a smooth path.

Psalm 27:11

Can our lives be different? Can we know for sure that we will go to Heaven when we die? The answer is yes—and the reason is because of what Jesus Christ did for us. We can have our sins forgiven, and we can begin life again by God's grace. Our journey through life can be different by traveling a new path—God's path.

Even before time began, God knew all about us and planned this new path for us. He looked across the ages and saw that we would be helpless and lost in sin, unable to find the right road on our own. He saw you. From all eternity He planned to provide another way—a way that will take us to Heaven someday and gives us purpose and peace in the meantime. That way is Jesus, who alone could say, "I am the way and the truth and the life. No one comes to the Father except through me" (John 14:6 NIV).

Sin has put us firmly on the wrong path. But because of Jesus, we can be firmly on the right path—and that's what we need.

Avoiding Life's Pitfalls

I have chosen the way of truth.

Psalm 119:30

Are we destined to lurch down life's road from one pothole or detour to another? Down inside we all sense that this was not the way life was meant to be, and we yearn for something better. We suspect there must be another way, a different path from the one we have been traveling. But why do so few people seem to find it? Why have we missed it? Can life be any different?

The answer to that last question is yes! No matter who you are or what your life has been like so far, the rest of your life's journey can be different. With God's help you can begin again. With Him you can confront your problems and begin to deal with them, and you can avoid life's pitfalls and detours. More than that, with God's help you can make an impact on our world. If you have never done so, ask Jesus Christ into your life today.

Joy and Peace

"You shall go out with joy,
And be led out with peace;
The mountains and the hills
Shall break forth into singing before you,
And all the trees of the field shall clap their hands."

Isaiah 55:12

Whatever has happened in your life so far—both good and bad—cannot be altered, and all the decisions and events that have made you what you are today are indelibly inscribed in the story of your life.

But with God's help you can change the future. The future doesn't need to be a copy of the past, nor does God want it to be. No matter what your life has been like so far, God wants to put your feet on a new path, a better path— His path. And regardless of what you may have thought, His path promises joy and peace and purpose far beyond anything you could have imagined. Which path are you on today—your path or God's path?

CONFIDENT *in* GOD'S LOVE

The love of God has been poured out in our hearts by the Holy Spirit who was given to us.

ROMANS 5:5

God—Our Mighty Rock

"No one is holy like the LORD,
For there is none besides You,
Nor is there any rock like our God."

1 SAMUEL 2:2

Just as a careful builder first lays a solid foundation before constructing a building, so God's Word gives us a solid foundation for building our spiritual lives.

The Bible says, "For no one can lay any foundation other than the one already laid, which is Jesus Christ" (1 Corinthians 3:11 NIV).

Why is this important? Because if we aren't sure whether or not God loves us, our journey through life will be hesitant, uncertain, insecure. But if we have confidence in God's love, then our journey will be joyful, assured, and filled with hope. A true Christian isn't prideful or arrogant; his confidence is not in himself but in God, and he humbly trusts Him every day. With the Psalmist he says, "My salvation and my honor depend on God; he is my mighty rock, my refuge" (Psalm 62:7 NIV). Is Christ the foundation of your life?

COMPLETE CONSECRATION

"Whoever desires to come after Me, let him deny himself."

MARK 8:34

Today Christ is calling Christians to cleansing—to dedication—to consecration—to full surrender. If you are a Christian and have been suffering defeat or have been living outside the will of God, I beg you to surrender every area of your life to Christ. Only surrendered Christians will make an impact on our world. The world does not need any more lukewarm Christians, or lazy Christians, or quarrelsome Christians, or doubting Christians, or prideful Christians. The Bible says, "a double minded man is unstable in all his ways" (James 1:8 KJV). What keeps you from a full surrender of your life to the King of kings and the Lord of lords?

Your response will make the difference between success and failure in your spiritual life. It will make the difference between your needing help and being able to help others. It will revolutionize your habits, your prayer life, your Bible reading, your giving, your testimony, and your church relationship. This is the Christian's hour of decision!

God Is Gracious

The grace of God that brings salvation has appeared to all men.

TITUS 2:11

One reason many Christians aren't sure of their salvation is because they still sin, and they fear God may reject them because of it. "God must be very disappointed in me," one man wrote me. "I don't see how I can still be a Christian when I keep losing my temper."

Sin is serious. But even when we sin, the Bible says, "The LORD is gracious and compassionate, slow to anger and rich in love" (Psalm 145:8 NIV). Suppose someone gave you a computer for your birthday. "This is my gift to you," they said, and you thanked them for being so generous. But suppose they added, "However, I have one requirement. Although I know you've never had a computer before, if you make a mistake on it—even one—then I'm going to take it back. You can't keep this computer unless you're perfect!" What would you think?

Yet many people assume God is like that: giving us the gift of salvation—then taking it back if we aren't perfect. But it isn't true.

GOD CARES FOR YOU

God is not the author of confusion but of peace.

1 CORINTHIANS 14:33

Who of us has not asked in times of affliction and difficulty, "Does God care for me?" The Psalmist said, "Refuge failed me; no man cared for my soul" (Psalm 142:4 KJV). Martha, overconcerned with her workaday duties, said to Jesus, "Lord, do You not care?" (Luke 10:40). How many faithful, loving mothers, overwhelmed by the burdens of motherhood, have cried anxiously, "Lord, do You not care?"

That question is forever answered in those reassuring words of Peter: "He cares for you" (1 Peter 5:7). This is the Word of God. Even if the world passes away, it will not change. You can be confident God cares for you. If He didn't, would He have sent Christ into the world to die for you? Of course not! That is why you can always turn to Him for the strength and encouragement you need.

Yes, life can be overwhelming at times. But when it is, remember this: God knows what you are facing, and "He cares for you."

CONFIDENT IN CHRIST ALONE

*A man is not justified by the works of the law but by
faith in Jesus Christ.*

GALATIANS 2:16

God doesn't save us because of who we are or how good
we are, nor can we ever claim we are better than others—because we aren't. God has saved us solely by His
mercy and grace, and we can't take any credit for our
salvation—none at all. The Bible says, "For it is by grace
you have been saved, through faith—and this not from
yourselves, it is the gift of God—not by works, so that no
one can boast" (Ephesians 2:8–9 NIV). God's grace—His
goodness and love toward us in spite of our sin—is the
wellspring of our salvation.

Our confidence must be in Christ and Christ alone. The
Bible says, "God has given us eternal life, and this life is in
his Son. He who has the Son has life; he who does not have
the Son of God does not have life" (1 John 5:11–12).

ABIDING PEACE

Fear not, for I am with you;
Be not dismayed, for I am your God.

ISAIAH 41:10

Whenever I think of God's faithfulness in the midst of suffering I am reminded of my dear late friend Corrie ten Boom, the remarkable Dutch woman who (with her family) hid Jews from the Nazis. After being imprisoned in Ravensbrük, the infamous concentration camp, Corrie traveled the world telling her story of suffering, forgiveness, and joy.

For thirty-five years she never had a permanent home, but when she was eighty-five and in declining health, some friends provided her with a lovely house in California. It was a luxury she never dreamed she would have (and one she never would have pursued on her own).

One day her friend, the late movie director James Collier, was visiting. He said, "Corrie, hasn't God been good to give you this beautiful house?" She replied firmly, "Jimmy, God was good when I was in Ravensbrük, too!" Most of us will never experience the horrors Corrie knew. But no matter what we face, we can depend on God's promise: "Fear not; for I am with you" (Isaiah 41:10).

A Settled Assurance

The work of righteousness will be peace,
and the effect of righteousness, quietness and assurance forever.

Isaiah 32:17

God has given us an inner witness to assure us of our salvation: the witness of the Holy Spirit. This witness within us isn't just an emotional feeling (although emotions may play a part). Instead, the Spirit's witness is a settled, inner conviction that the Gospel is true, and we now belong to Christ.

This is somewhat like being a member of a family. Sometimes you may feel very close to your family; sometimes you may not. But down inside you always know you are part of that family, whether you feel close to them or not. You know you belong to each other; you have a settled, inner conviction that isn't just an emotional feeling. In fact, it isn't based on your feelings at all. It is based on a fact—the fact that you were born into that family. In the same way, the Holy Spirit gives us an inner, settled conviction that we have been born into a family—the family of God, who is our Heavenly Father.

Our Loving, Compassionate God

I am the bread of life.

JOHN 6:35

Jesus came to the world so we could know, once and for all, that God is concerned about the way we live, the way we believe, and the way we die. God could have told us in other ways, of course—and He had, throughout the pages of the Old Testament and in the lives of His people. By His written Word, He declared His love.

But Jesus was the Living Word. By His life, death, and resurrection, Jesus demonstrated God's love in a way we could never deny. Paul wrote, "But God demonstrates His own love toward us, in that while we were still sinners, Christ died for us" (Romans 5:8).

Every time He fed the hungry, He was saying, "I am the bread of life." Every time He healed a suffering person, He was saying, "It hurts Me to see you in pain." Every move He made, every miracle He performed, every word He spoke was for the purpose of reconciling a lost world to the loving, compassionate God.

God Is with Us

"The Helper, the Holy Spirit, whom the Father will send in My name, He will teach you all things, and bring to your remembrance all things that I said to you."

John 14:26

When we come to Christ, God Himself comes to live within us by His Holy Spirit. We are not alone; God is with us!

If you know Christ, you don't need to beg for the Holy Spirit to come into your life; He is already there—whether you "feel" His presence or not. Don't confuse the Holy Spirit with an emotional feeling or a particular type of spiritual experience. Instead, accept by faith what God has promised: when you come to Christ, the Holy Spirit comes to live within you.

Why has God given us the Holy Spirit? The Spirit has been given for many reasons—but one is to help us live the way we should. God has given us a new purpose—but without a new power we'll never be able to achieve it.

We are too weak! But the Bible says, "The Spirit helps us in our weakness" (Romans 8:26 NIV). We aren't meant to live the Christian life in our own strength. God has provided His Spirit to help us.

A COMPLETE SACRIFICE

He has appeared to put away sin by the sacrifice of Himself.

HEBREWS 9:26

You and I can't add anything to what Christ did for us, because He has done it all. If Christ's death was not enough . . . if we needed to add our own good works to His in order to be saved . . . then we could never know for sure that we will go to Heaven when we die, because we could never be sure if we have done enough. But the ransom has been fully paid, and Christ's work is finished.

Nothing more remains to be done. Christ's sacrifice is complete! His work on your behalf is finished! Pause right now and thank Him for making you part of His family forever.

A CERTAIN HOPE

"Blessed is the man who trusts in the LORD,
And whose hope is the LORD."

JEREMIAH 17:7

One of the great hymns of the church, "The Solid Rock," by Edward Mote and William Bradbury, begins, "My hope is built on nothing less, than Jesus' blood and righteousness; I dare not trust the sweetest frame, but wholly lean on Jesus' name. On Christ, the solid Rock, I stand; all other ground is sinking sand."

On what is your hope built? You may hope for a raise in pay at work. You may hope that you pass an exam at school. You may even hope that you win a contest you have entered. Such hopes are based on externals over which we have little control: a favorable view of our work by the boss, the "right" questions being asked by the professor, our name being drawn among thousands of entries.

But all these "hopes" fade into insignificance when compared with the greatest hope of all—our hope of salvation in Christ. And that hope is an absolute certainty, because it is based not on ourselves or our good works, but squarely on "Jesus' blood and righteousness."

A Family Resemblance

All of you be of one mind, having compassion for one
another; love as brothers, be tenderhearted, be courteous.

1 Peter 3:8

God's will is for us to become more and more like Christ.
It is that simple—and also that complex.

Perhaps you've had the experience of having someone
come up to you and say, "You look just like your mother!"
or "You look just like your brother!" They saw a family
resemblance between you and your parents or some other
member of your family. Grandparents often spend hours
trying to decide who a newborn baby resembles in the
family (usually with little success!). You may even have
seen married couples who looked more and more like
each other as the years went by.

In a far deeper way, God's will is that we would bear
a family resemblance to His Son. In other words, God's
plan is for us to become more and more like Jesus—not
physically, of course, but in the way we think and act and
treat other people. Is this your goal?

PERFECT PEACE

"Your faith has saved you. Go in peace."

LUKE 7:50

During the First World War, on Christmas Eve, the battlefield was strangely quiet. As the soft snow fell, the thoughts of the young men were of home and family.

Softly one lad began to hum "Silent Night." Others took up the chorus until the trenches resounded with the Christmas song. When they finished, they were astonished to hear the song echoing from the trenches across no-man's-land: in their own tongue the other soldiers also sang "Silent Night." That night they were thinking of the Prince of Peace, the Christ of Christmas.

How different this world would be if we could unite together around that "Holy Infant so tender and mild." Earth can be as Heaven with Christ. Discord can be as peace when Christ is near. Midnight gloom can be transformed into noonday brightness when He abides with us. Full peace will come only when Christ returns. But until that day we can know His peace in our hearts and can be messengers of His peace in the world, as we commit our lives to Him.

Lord of All

> *"If anyone desires to come after Me, let him deny himself, and take up his cross daily, and follow Me."*
>
> LUKE 9:23

God's will is for you to become more and more like Christ right where you are. Jesus didn't isolate Himself from daily life; He became involved in people's lives wherever He went. At times He withdrew to rest and spend time alone with His Heavenly Father—and so should we. But Jesus also knew what it was to live under pressure, and yet He never wavered from God's plan for His life. Neither should we.

How do we become more like Christ? How does it happen? It happens as we submit every area of our lives to His authority. Nothing must be excluded from His influence, and nothing must be withheld from His control. Many years ago I heard someone use a little phrase I have never forgotten: "If Christ is to be Lord at all, then He must be Lord of all."

63

Peace in the Storm

May the God of hope fill you with all joy and peace.

Romans 15:13

A wonderful old hymn says, "He gives us peace in the midst of a storm." In life we face all kinds of storms. We usually think of the personal "storms" that come our way—financial worries, problems in our marriage or family, illness, the betrayal of a friend, and so forth. But we face other kinds of storms that threaten to engulf us also: storms of materialism, storms of secularism, storms of moral degeneracy, storms of injustice, terrorism, and war.

Do you remember the violent storm that came upon Jesus and His disciples one night on the Sea of Galilee? His disciples grew panicky—but Jesus stayed fast asleep. He was at peace because He knew God was in control. He was at peace also because He was sovereign over the storm, and He knew it would vanish at His Word: "Peace, be still!" (Mark 4:39).

His Word still calms the turmoil in our lives. Is some storm making you fearful today? Stay close to Jesus, for His Word brings peace.

Pleasing and Perfect

You were bought at a price; therefore glorify God in
your body and in your spirit, which are God's.

1 Corinthians 6:20

People saw in Jesus a quality of life they had never seen before, and they wanted to experience it for themselves. When they looked at Him, they saw joy and peace and kindness—and most of all, they saw God's love.

God wants to give us that same quality of life—the life of Jesus. Jesus said to His disciples, "I have told you this so that my joy may be in you and that your joy may be complete" (John 15:11 NIV).

God's plan is to remake us from within, by His Holy Spirit. The Bible says, "Do not conform to the pattern of this world, but be transformed by the renewing of your mind. Then you will be able to test and approve what God's will is—his good, pleasing and perfect will" (Romans 12:2 NIV).

That's what God's will is like: good, pleasing, and perfect. Why settle for anything less?

GOD NEVER CHANGES

"God is Spirit, and those who worship Him must worship in spirit and truth."

JOHN 4:24

I was reared in a small Presbyterian church in Charlotte, North Carolina. Before I was ten years of age, my mother made me memorize the "Shorter Catechism," a summary of basic Christian beliefs in the form of questions and answers. In the catechism, we were asked to define God. The answer we learned was, "God is a Spirit—infinite, eternal, and unchangeable."

Those three words beautifully describe God. He is infinite—not body-bound. Eternal—He has no beginning and no ending. He is unchangeable—never changing, never unreliable. As the Bible says, with God "there is no variation or shadow of turning" (James 1:17).

People change, fashions change, conditions and circumstances change, but God never changes. His love never changes. His holiness never changes. His purpose never changes. His glory never changes. He is the same yesterday, today, and forever. Can you think of any reason not to trust Him? Neither can I!

LORD AND MASTER

"You call Me Teacher and Lord, and you say well, for so I am."

I wonder if you've ever thought about the incredible number of messages that rain down on us every day: television ads, e-mails, phone calls, magazines, junk mail, videos, billboards, conversations—the list is almost endless.

How many of those shape our thinking? How many of them subtly convince us that the road to happiness is really paved with possessions, or beauty, or money, or fame, or any of a hundred other things? How many of them persuade us that the most important thing in life is financial success, or the esteem of others, or power, or sex? It's hard to resist the cumulative impact of so many messages.

But God says our thinking must be shaped by His truth. What this world calls valuable, God calls worthless. What this world scorns, God exalts. "My thoughts are not your thoughts, nor are your ways My ways" (Isaiah 55:8). Jesus said, "You call me Teacher and Lord, and you say well, for so I am" (John 13:13). Is He your Teacher and Lord—or is the world?

THE ANTHEM OF HIS NAME

God also has . . . given Him the name which is above
every name.

PHILIPPIANS 2:9

Over two thousand years ago, on a night the world has come to call Christmas, a young Jewish maiden went through the experience countless mothers had before her: she brought forth a child. But this birth was like no other in the history of the human race. For one thing, this Child had no human father. As the angel had promised, "The Holy Spirit will come upon you, and the power of the Highest will overshadow you" (Luke 1:35). In humble obedience the Virgin Mary responded, "Let it be to me according to your word" (Luke 1:38).

But it also was like no other birth because of the One who was born. This was no ordinary child. This was the unique Son of God, sent from Heaven to save us from our sins. Amid the glitter and busyness of the season, don't lose sight of the miracle of that first Christmas. With the wise men, let us fall down and worship Him (Matthew 2:11).

SERVING GOD FOREVER

Because of His great love . . . He . . . made us alive together with Christ.

EPHESIANS 2:4–5

Your life may seem monotonous and filled with drudgery. Yet remember, if you are a Christian, you are not working for an hour or for a day but for eternity. When this body of corruption shall take on immortality, another part of our work will begin, for the Scripture teaches that God's servants shall serve Him forever. The difference is that in Heaven we will never grow bored or weary!

Some time ago a man said to me, "You might be mistaken, for no one has ever come back from the grave to tell us." I replied, "Sir, that's exactly where you are wrong. Someone has returned—His name is Jesus Christ, our Lord."

That makes all the difference! Because Christ is alive, we have "an inheritance incorruptible and undefiled . . . reserved in heaven" (1 Peter 1:4). And this helps us persevere, even when life seems dull.

Our Great Assurance

*Let us draw near with a true heart in full assurance
of faith.*

Hebrews 10:22

Disregard your feelings when you come to Christ. You aren't saved by your feelings; you are saved by Christ. Feelings come and go, but Christ remains.

Only the facts matter—the fact that Jesus Christ died for your sins and rose again; the fact that if you have committed your life to Him, He has promised to forgive you and save you. The Bible says, "God has given us eternal life, and this life is in His Son. He who has the Son has life" (1 John 5:11–12).

That is God's promise to you—and He cannot lie. Your feelings will lie to you—and Satan may even use them to convince you God has abandoned you or that you have lost your salvation. But remember: "There is no truth in him. When he lies, he speaks his native language, for he is a liar and the father of lies" (John 8:44 NIV).

How wonderful to know our faith is based on God's truth, and not our feelings!

GOD'S ABIDING PRESENCE

The love of God has been poured out in our hearts by
the Holy Spirit who was given to us.

ROMANS 5:5

Years ago when I traveled to Europe to preach, I liked to travel by sea, to enjoy the five days of relative quiet on the ship.

On one of my voyages, Captain Anderson of the United States took me down to see the ship's gyroscope. He said, "When the sea is rough, the gyroscope helps to keep the ship on an even keel. Though the waves may reach tremendous proportions, the gyroscope helps to stabilize the vessel and maintain a high degree of equilibrium."

As I listened, I thought how like the gyroscope is the Holy Spirit in our hearts. Let the storms of life break over our heads. Let the enemy Satan come in like a flood. Let the waves of sorrow, suffering, temptation, and testing be unleashed upon us. Our souls will be kept on an even keel and in perfect peace when the Holy Spirit dwells in our hearts. He comforts us with God's abiding presence, and assures us that God's promises are true.

GROWING *in* GOD'S LOVE

*He will love you and bless
you and multiply you.*

DEUTERONOMY 7:13

WE NEED GOD'S POWER

Thanks be to God who always leads us in triumph in Christ, and through us diffuses the fragrance of His knowledge in every place.

2 CORINTHIANS 2:14

As humans we have two great spiritual needs. The first is forgiveness, which God made possible by sending His Son into the world to die for our sins. Our second need, however, is for goodness, which God also made possible by sending the Holy Spirit to dwell within us.

If we are to live the way God meant us to live . . . if we are to become more like Christ . . . if we are to travel our journey wisely . . . then we need both God's forgiveness and goodness. We need the work of the Son for us, and we need the work of the Holy Spirit in us. To the great gift of forgiveness God adds the great gift of the Holy Spirit. As a friend of mine once said, "I need Jesus Christ for my eternal life, and the Holy Spirit of God for my internal life."

Triumph Through Trust

Neither death nor life . . . nor things present nor things to come . . . shall be able to separate us from the love of God.

ROMANS 8:38-39

There are two ways to respond to adversity: discouragement or trust. The problem with giving in to discouragement is that it only makes things worse, for with it may come bitterness, anger, jealousy, revenge, and so forth. We may even try to escape through drugs or alcohol. But do any of these solve the problem? No! God has a better way: the way of trust. Sometimes He may show us that we were in the wrong. When that is the case, we need to confess, repent, and seek His forgiveness. Sometimes, however, we can only accept what is happening and ask God to help us endure it and triumph over it.

One of the best ways to overcome adversity, I've found, is to praise God right in the middle of the turmoil. Turning to God's Word will also encourage us; many of the Psalms, for example, were written in the midst of suffering and adversity. Follow the Psalmist's example: "Bless the LORD, O my soul, and forget not all His benefits" (Psalm 103:2).

FAITH GROWS BY EXPRESSION

"You are the light of the world."

MATTHEW 5:14

Tom Allan, Scotland's famous preacher, was brought to Christ while a soldier was singing, "Were you there when they crucified my Lord?" He said it was neither the song nor the voice, but the spirit in which that soldier sang—something about his manner, something about his sincerity of expression—that convicted Allan of his wicked life and turned him to the Savior.

Jesus said, "You are the light of the world. . . . Let your light so shine before [others], that they may see your good works and glorify your Father in heaven" (Matthew 5:14, 16).

Our faith becomes stronger as we express it; a growing faith is a sharing faith. Pray now for those you know who need Christ, and ask God to help you be a witness to them—by the life you live and the words you speak.

Changed by God's Spirit

"When He, the Spirit of truth, has come, He will guide
you into all truth."

John 16:13

Many Christians know they should be better persons, and they struggle with all their might to change their behavior. But most of their attempts at self-improvement fail, and they end up frustrated and discouraged. They can echo the words of the Apostle Paul: "I have the desire to do what is good, but I cannot carry it out. For I do not do the good I want to do, but the evil I do not want to do—this I keep on doing" (Romans 7:18–19 NIV).

What is the problem? The problem is that we are relying on our own strength instead of the strength of the Holy Spirit. We not only need to know how God wants us to live, but we also need the power to achieve it. And God has given us that power by giving us His Holy Spirit. He gives us the Bible to teach us, and other Christians to encourage us—but He also gives us His Spirit to change us. Not only do we have other Christians around us, but we also have the Holy Spirit within us. He is our constant, unchanging companion on the journey.

Life-Giving Water

My soul thirsts for You;
My flesh longs for You
In a dry and thirsty land.

Psalm 63:1

The water for our home in the mountains of North Carolina comes from a spring above the house. When we moved there, the old-timers in the area told us this particular spring would always flow, even in the worst drought—and they were right. One year, however, we had an abnormally cold winter, and one day we found ourselves without water. Ice had formed in the pipe running from the spring, and we had to dig through the frozen ground and use a blowtorch to melt it. Only then did the flow resume.

I have often compared that spring to the Holy Spirit. No matter the circumstances, the Holy Spirit's flow is always available to us—just like that spring. But sin is like the ice that blocked our pipe. We allow the spiritual coldness of a hostile world to freeze our souls and cut off the Spirit's life-giving water.

If your spiritual life is dry and barren, begin by praying the Psalmist's prayer: "Search me, O God, and know my heart . . . . See if there is any offensive way in me" (Psalm 139:23–24 NIV).

A New Start Each Day

Draw near to God and He will draw near to you.

Being filled with the Holy Spirit isn't a once-for-all event, but a continuous reality every day of our lives. Is it for you?

Personally I find it helpful to begin each day by silently committing it to God (even before I get up), thanking Him that I belong to Him, and that He knows what the day holds for me. Then I ask Him to use me that day for His glory and to cleanse me from every sin that might hinder this.

Then I step out in faith, believing His Spirit will fill me as I obey His Word and trust in Him. I won't always be aware of His presence, but at the end of the day I know I'll be able to look back and thank Him for being with me and guiding me. He promised to be with me that day— and He was.

This can be your experience also, as you yield your life daily to Christ's Lordship. Give each day to Him, so that at its end you can look back and thank Him for being with you, as He promised.

TRUE THANKSGIVING

Oh, give thanks to the LORD, for He is good!

PSALM 107:1

Separated from friends, unjustly accused, brutally treated—if any man had a right to complain it was this man, languishing almost forgotten in a harsh Roman prison. But instead of complaints, his lips rang with words of praise and thanksgiving!

This was the apostle Paul—a man who had learned the meaning of true thanksgiving, even in the midst of great adversity. Look carefully at what he wrote during that prison experience: "Sing and make music from your heart to the Lord, always giving thanks to God the Father for everything, in the name of our Lord Jesus Christ" (Ephesians 5:19–20 NIV).

Think of it! "Always giving thanks . . . for everything" no matter the circumstances. His guards and fellow prisoners must have thought him crazy—but that didn't stop him. Thanksgiving for Paul was not a once-a-year celebration, but a daily reality that made him a joyful person in every situation. May that be true of us.

GOD CARES

The eyes of the LORD are on the righteous,
And His ears are open to their cry.

PSALM 34:15

One of God's most comforting promises is that we can bring every need and burden to Him: "Cast your cares on the LORD and he will sustain you; he will never let the righteous be shaken" (Psalm 55:22 NIV). The Bible also says, "The prayer of a righteous person is powerful and effective" (James 5:16 NIV). Some of my strongest memories of our trips to Africa and India were the prayer meetings we attended—sometimes with thousands gathered in the early morning. I have seldom heard such fervent prayer, and the reason was because they deeply believed prayer is "powerful and effective." God's Word is filled with promises about prayer, and repeatedly He tells us to bring our burdens to Him.

In fact, God urges us to bring our concerns to Him—not just petitions about our own needs, but also intercessions for others. Just as an earthly father wants his children to come to him with their requests, so our Heavenly Father wants us to come to Him.

STRENGTH TO FACE TEMPTATION

Put on the whole armor of God, that you may be able to stand against the wiles of the devil.

EPHESIANS 6:11

Temptation isn't the same thing as sin, and it isn't a sin to be tempted. Temptation is being enticed to do wrong; sin is actually doing it. It isn't a sin to be tempted, but it is a sin to give in to the temptation. At the beginning of His ministry "Jesus was led by the Spirit into the wilderness to be tempted by the devil" (Matthew 4:1 NIV). But Jesus didn't give in to Satan's temptations (although they were very intense and alluring). The Bible says Jesus was "tempted in every way, just as we are—yet he did not sin" (Hebrews 4:15 NIV).

Whenever I am tempted to do something wrong, I gain great strength from those words about Jesus. You and I will never face a temptation He doesn't understand, for He was tempted "in every way, just as we are." He knows what we are going through when we are tempted, because He has already been there. But He also points the way to victory, because He faced temptation's challenge—and overcame it. So can we.

A Clear Distinction

*Blessed is the man who endures temptation; for when
he has been approved, he will receive the crown of life
which the Lord has promised to those who love Him.*

JAMES 1:12

We need to know what the Bible teaches about right and
wrong. Every day we are battered by messages—from the
media, advertising, entertainment, celebrities, even our
friends—with one underlying message: "Live for yourself."
The world hammers away at us, trying to shape us into its
mold and make us believe that sin isn't really sin. After all,
isn't everyone doing it? But God says, "Do not conform to
the pattern of this world, but be transformed by the renewing of your mind" (Romans 12:2 NIV).

Ask God to help you recognize temptation when it
comes. When you are unsure whether or not something
is wrong, ask yourself these questions: Does this glorify
God? Does it draw me closer to Christ, or does it make
me preoccupied with this world? Will it harm my health
or hurt me in some other way? Will it cause someone else
to stumble spiritually or morally (especially a less mature
Christian)? I have never forgotten what a wise Christian
said to me many years ago: "When in doubt—don't!"

God's "Love Letter"

Be doers of the word, and not hearers only.

JAMES 1:22

The Bible isn't just for preachers and scholars! God wants to speak to you through His Word, and no matter who you are, the Bible can come alive to you. You may never understand everything in the Bible, but you can understand something.

Bible reading shouldn't be a burden but a joy! I vividly remember the day I received Ruth's letter saying she had decided to accept my proposal for marriage. I probably read and reread it dozens of times that day! God wants to talk with us through His Word—in fact, it is His "love letter" to us. Why shouldn't we come to it joyfully?

Ask God to speak to you through its pages—and then expect Him to do so. This doesn't mean every time we open the Bible we'll find something new; God may be underlining truths we already know. But let the Psalmist's prayer become yours: "Open my eyes that I may see wonderful things in your law" (Psalm 119:18 NIV).

GOD'S DEPENDABLE WORD

"I am the LORD, I do not change."

MALACHI 3:6

From time to time, children write me with their questions about God. One favorite question is this: Is there anything God can't do? I always answer "yes." The one thing God can't do, I explain, is anything wrong. For example, I add, God can never tell a lie—and because of that, we can trust whatever He promises us in His Word, the Bible.

From one end of the Bible to the other God assures us that He will never go back on His promises. Make them the foundation of your life every day.

The Gift of Prayer

Trust in Him at all times, you people;
Pour out your heart before Him;
God is a refuge for us.

Psalm 62:8

Central to any relationship is communication. It's true on a human level; what kind of relationship do two people have who never talk with each other? In a far greater way, our relationship with God involves communication—not just an occasional brief chat, but a deep sharing of ourselves and our concerns with God. Because Christ has opened Heaven's door for us, the Bible says, we should "approach God's throne of grace with confidence, so that we may receive mercy and find grace to help us in our time of need" (Hebrews 4:16 NIV).

In the Bible, God speaks to us; in prayer we speak to God. Both are essential—and both are gifts God has given us so we can know each other. Prayer is a gift from God's hand just as much as the Bible, and He has given us the privilege of prayer because He loves us and wants our fellowship.

A Person of Prayer

Cast your burden on the LORD,
And He shall sustain you;

PSALM 55:22

Every man or woman whose life has ever counted for God has been a person of prayer. Jesus demonstrated the importance of prayer by His own example. His whole ministry was saturated with prayer. On one occasion, "Jesus got up, left the house and went off to a solitary place, where he prayed" (Mark 1:35 NIV). On another occasion "Jesus was praying in a certain place. When he finished, one of his disciples said to him, 'Lord, teach us to pray'" (Luke 11:1 NIV). He responded by giving them the Lord's Prayer. As His death approached He withdrew to the Garden of Gethsemane, to pray, "And being in anguish, he prayed more earnestly, and his sweat was like drops of blood falling to the ground" (Luke 22:44 NIV). His last words from the cross were a prayer: "Father, into your hands I commit my spirit" (Luke 23:46 NIV).

If prayer was this important to the Son of God, shouldn't it be important to us?

A DECLARATION OF DEPENDENCE

"Your will be done
On earth as it is in heaven."

MATTHEW 6:10

A friend of mine likes to define prayer as "a declaration of dependence"—and he has a point. We will only pray when we realize how dependent we are on God, and we trust Him to hear our prayers and answer them according to His will. Recently I saw a documentary on television about the bombing of London during the Second World War. One man in the program said that when the bombs began to fall, he began praying for the first time in his life. I'm sure the same is true for countless people who never think about God but suddenly find themselves in a crisis that is beyond them and cry out for help. They are realizing—even if dimly—that they are dependent on God after all.

God wants us to bring our every concern to Him in prayer, and to be persistent in our praying.

GIVING THANKS TO GOD

Praise the LORD!
For it is good to sing praises to our God;
For it is pleasant, and praise is beautiful.

PSALM 147:1

When we praise God, our focus is on Him, not on ourselves. Many of the Psalms are actually prayers, and it is no accident that the word *praise* occurs in the book of Psalms over one hundred times.

The Bible says, "Enter his gates with thanksgiving and his courts with praise; give thanks to him and praise his name" (Psalm 100:4 NIV).

Why should we give thanks? One reason is because everything we have comes from God: "Every good and perfect gift is from above, coming down from the Father" (James 1:17 NIV). We can't take credit for anything—even our successes. God gave us our abilities; He arranged our circumstances; He blessed our efforts. Therefore, the Bible says, "Give thanks to the LORD, for he is good; his love endures forever" (Psalm 106:1 NIV). Make thankfulness a part of your life, today and always.

Prayer and Praise

I will bless the LORD at all times;
His praise shall continually be in my mouth.

PSALM 34:1

If all we do is ask God for things we want, our prayers quickly become selfish. Although the thought might shock us, we begin to think of God as little more than a glorified Santa Claus to whom we turn only when we want something. But God is far greater than this. Remember: God isn't our servant; we are His servants.

True prayer begins by seeing God as He really is—and that is why praise should be a regular part of our prayers. When we praise God, our focus is on Him, not on ourselves.

You are a child of God if you know Christ, and He welcomes your prayers. He is much more concerned about our hearts than our eloquence.

Part of God's Family

The things that you have heard from me among many witnesses, commit these to faithful men who will be able to teach others also.

2 Timothy 2:2

We not only belong to God; we also belong to each other. We aren't traveling alone on this journey God has given; others are traveling it with us. But unlike a race or a marathon, we aren't competing with each other or trying to get ahead of them and win. We are traveling together on this journey, sharing its joys and bearing each other's burdens and heartaches. If someone stumbles, we help them get to their feet; if someone veers off course, we urge them back. On this journey we are all brothers and sisters in the same family—the family of God.

This family is what the New Testament calls the Church. In its fullest sense "the Church" isn't just a particular building or congregation, but the spiritual fellowship of all who belong to Jesus Christ. If we belong to Christ, we also belong to each other; if we have committed our lives to Him, we are also committed to each other. The reason is simple: we need each other.

The Gift of Each Other

Let the word of Christ dwell in you richly in all wisdom,
teaching and admonishing one another in psalms and
hymns and spiritual songs, singing with grace in your
hearts to the Lord.

Colossians 3:16

The word *Church* in the Bible refers to the company of all believers, who are spiritually united by their relationship with Christ. The Church includes all believers everywhere—even those who have died and are now in Heaven. As my mother approached death, she wasn't only looking forward to being with Christ, but also being reunited with friends and family who had already entered Heaven. If you belong to Christ, you are part of this great invisible fellowship of believers across the ages.

The Bible is God's gift to you—but your fellow Christians are His gift to you also. One of the main tools God uses to shape us and make us more like Christ is our fellowship with other Christians. In fact, unless we have active contact with other believers our spiritual lives will be stunted. The Bible says, "As iron sharpens iron, so one person sharpens another" (Proverbs 27:17 NIV). Our fellowship with other believers is a gift from God.

Encouragement and Wisdom

Since we are receiving a kingdom
which cannot be shaken, let us have grace,
by which we may serve God acceptably
with reverence and godly fear.

Hebrews 12:28

We need each other's encouragement and wisdom. Sometimes we may encourage someone without even being aware of it. I can't begin to count the times I have heard a preacher or Bible teacher and said to myself afterward, "That message was exactly what I needed!" Even your example of attending church may encourage someone who is searching for God, although you may never know it.

We also encourage each other on a personal level. Some of my greatest encouragement over the years has come from godly friends who were willing to pray and share their wisdom with me. Whenever we are with other believers—whether in a church service with hundreds of people or just sharing a cup of coffee with a Christian friend—God can lift us up and increase our faith through their encouragement and counsel.

LIVING *in* GOD'S LOVE

*"He will quiet you with His love,
He will rejoice over you with
singing."*

ZEPHANIAH 3:17

A Whole New Life

*Be renewed in the spirit of your mind, and . . . put on
the new man which was created according to God, in
true righteousness and holiness.*

EPHESIANS 4:23–24

When we come to Christ, God gives us a whole new life:
a new relationship, a new citizenship, a new family, a new
purpose, a new power, a new destiny.

But this isn't the end of His bounty, for God also gives
us one final gift: a new journey—a whole new path to follow until the day He takes us to Heaven.

Coming to Christ isn't an end but a beginning—the
beginning of a whole new life. We aren't only called to
become Christians; we are also called to be Christians.
Don't ever think that faith in Christ is just a type of "spiritual life insurance"—something we obtain and then put
away until we need it to get into Heaven. The Christian life
is a new journey—one that will take us the rest of our lives.

And the best part is this: we never walk it alone, for
Christ walks with us.

TRUST AND OBEY

Blessed is that man who makes the LORD his trust.

PSALM 40:4

Some years ago someone gave my little boy a dollar. He brought it to me and said, "Daddy, keep this for me." But in a few minutes, he came back and said, "Daddy, I'd better keep my own dollar." He tucked it in his pocket and went out to play. In a few minutes, he came back with tears in his eyes, saying, "Daddy, I lost my dollar. Help me find it."

How often we commit our burdens to the Lord and then fail to trust Him by taking matters into our own hands. Then, when we have messed things up, we pray, "Oh, Lord, help me, I'm in trouble."

The choice is yours. Do you want to trust your life in God's "pocket" or keep it in your own? The Bible's promise is true: "Blessed is that man who makes the Lord his trust."

GOD'S RICH RESOURCES

I can do all things through Christ who strengthens me.

PHILIPPIANS 4:13

Our journey—our race—lasts as long as God gives us life, and we aren't meant to wander off the track, or quit and join the spectators, or decide we'll just slow down and take it easy while others pass us by. Our example is Jesus, who "for the joy set before him endured the cross, scorning its shame, and sat down at the right hand of the throne of God" (Hebrews 12:2 NIV). He faithfully ran the race God had prepared for Him, even at the cost of His own blood.

God didn't intend for us to travel our journey in our own strength anyway, but only with the strength He supplies. I am convinced the main reason so many Christians become spiritually discouraged and defeated is because they have never discovered this truth. They assume it must be up to them to live the Christian life, and they never make use of the rich resources God has already provided to strengthen us for the journey. Like a guest who has been invited to a banquet but never sits down to the meal, they have never learned to draw their strength from God's resources. Don't let this be true of you!

PURE IN HEART

"Blessed are the pure in heart, for they shall see God."

MATTHEW 5:8

Why does Jesus say we should be "pure in heart"? The reason is because our hearts—our inner beings—are the root of all our actions. From our hearts come our motives, our desires, our goals, our emotions. If our hearts aren't right, neither will be our actions. Jesus put it this way: "From within, out of the heart of men, proceed evil thoughts, adulteries, fornications, murders, thefts, covetousness, wickedness, deceit, lewdness, an evil eye, blasphemy, pride, foolishness" (Mark 7:21–22). Not a very pretty picture!

But God wants to give us a pure heart—and He will. He does this first of all when we turn to Christ in repentance and faith, for "the blood of Jesus Christ His Son cleanses us from all sin" (1 John 1:7). But He does it also day by day, as we submit to the Holy Spirit and—with His help—flee from evil and seek what is good.

To Be a Disciple

"If anyone loves Me, he will keep My word; and My Father will love him, and We will come to him and make Our home with him."

JOHN 14:23

Jesus said, "If you hold to my teaching, you are really my disciples" (John 8:31 NIV).

What is a disciple? A disciple is a learner or a student. The twelve whom Jesus called to be His closest companions were with Him day and night. They had a personal relationship with Him—walking with Him, eating with Him, sharing in His conversation, observing the way He lived, listening to Him preach to the crowds. But they weren't following Jesus just to enjoy His presence. As Jesus' disciples they had a purpose: to learn from Him—absorbing His teaching, learning from His example, even profiting from His rebukes. And this was true for all His disciples, not just the twelve. To be a disciple is to be a learner.

Pray Anywhere, Any Time

Rejoice always, pray without ceasing.

1 Thessalonians 5:16–17

Prayer is an essential part of a healthy Christian life. Just as omitting an essential vitamin from our diet will make us physically weak, so a lack of prayer will make us spiritually anemic.

The Bible says, "Pray without ceasing" (1 Thessalonians 5:17). It isn't enough to get out of bed in the morning, quickly bow our heads, and repeat a few sentences. Instead, we need to set aside specific times to be alone with God, speaking to Him in prayer and listening to Him speak through His Word. If you set aside special times for prayer, your unconscious mind will be saturated with prayer all day long.

For the overworked mother or other busy person this may seem impossible (although even a few minutes alone with God can reap rich rewards). But even when we are busy, we can "pray without ceasing" in our hearts and minds. We can pray anywhere, any time—and God will hear us. Today let prayer saturate your life "without ceasing."

Our Infinite God

Great is the LORD, and greatly to be praised.

PSALM 48:1

As a boy I grew up in the rural American South. My idea of the ocean was so small that the first time I saw the Atlantic I couldn't comprehend how any lake could be so big! The vastness of the ocean cannot be understood until it is seen. This is the same with God's love. It passes knowledge. Until you actually experience it, no one can describe its wonders to you.

Behind the love of God lies His omniscience—His ability to "know and understand all." Omniscience is a quality of God that is His alone. God possesses infinite knowledge and an awareness that is uniquely His. At all times, even in the midst of any type of suffering, I can realize that He knows, loves, watches, understands, and, more than that, has a purpose.

No matter what comes your way . . . no matter how tempted you are to give in to despair . . . never forget: God's love for you can never be exhausted, for His love is beyond measure.

PEACE WITH GOD

"Peace I leave with you, My peace I give to you . . . Let not your heart be troubled, neither let it be afraid."

JOHN 14:27

When we follow Christ, we have peace—an inner peace that comes from a deep and abiding trust in His promises. One dimension of this is our peace with God. When warring nations sign a peace treaty, the fighting between them stops—and this is what has happened between us and God. At one time we were at war with God, but now "we have peace with God through our Lord Jesus Christ" (Romans 5:1 NIV).

In addition, when we walk with Christ we have peace in our hearts. The wars that once raged in our hearts are ended. So do our conflicts with other people, and we come to have peace with others. When we know Christ, we truly have peace—peace with God, peace in our hearts, and peace with others.

This peace is real—just as real as God Himself. It is an inner peace—a peace in our souls and minds and emotions—that keeps us calm even in the midst of life's worst storms.

Look to God

"Lift up your heads, because your redemption draws near."

LUKE 21:28

If you've ever flown in an airplane you know that your perspective of the earth is far different from what it was when you were on the ground. Pictures of the earth that have been taken from the moon and from space show an earth that looks much different from what we see down here.

This is the kind of perspective God wants to give us concerning our lives. As we look to God, instead of to ourselves and our circumstances, our perspectives change. Don't get bogged down in the circumstances of life. At the moment we see only our immediate problems and burdens, but God sees the whole. He sees not only the present, but the future as well. He wants to lift us above ourselves. He wants us to see everything in light of His plans. The Psalmist said, "The LORD will perfect that which concerns me" (Psalm 138:8).

Don't get bogged down. Keep your eyes on God, for He sees the whole picture, and He knows what is best for you. You can trust Him, because He loves you.

NEAR TO GOD

"In the world you will have tribulation; but be of good cheer, I have overcome the world."

JOHN 16:33

The key to spiritual victory is to stay close to God. The Bible puts it this way: "Submit yourselves, then, to God. Resist the devil, and he will flee from you. Come near to God and he will come near to you" (James 4:7–8 NIV). Submit . . . resist . . . come near—this is what we must do if we are to gain spiritual victory.

If you know Christ, you have a personal relationship with God. God isn't a remote, forbidding figure who doesn't want anything to do with you. He is your loving Heavenly Father, and even now His Son is praying for you. Therefore, the Bible says, "let us draw near to God with a sincere heart with the full assurance that faith brings" (Hebrews 10:22 NIV). You can come near to God because He wants you to!

GOD'S PERFECT PLAN

*Be transformed . . . that you may prove what is that . . .
perfect will of God.*

ROMANS 12:2

The Bible reveals that God has a plan for every life, and that if we live in constant fellowship with Him, He will direct and lead us in the fulfillment of this plan.

God does not reveal His plan through fortune-tellers, astrologers, soothsayers, and workers of hocus-pocus. His perfect will is reserved for those who have trusted Christ for salvation. He shares His secrets only with those who are redeemed and transformed, and who humbly seek His will for their lives.

You cannot know the will of God for your life unless you first come to the cross and confess that you are a sinner and receive Christ as Lord and Savior. Once you do come to Him, you begin a whole new life—life not lived for yourself but for Christ. From that moment on God wants to show you His will. Whatever decisions you face today, commit them to God and ask Him to guide you—and He will.

BUILDING A STRONG FAITH

"If you have faith as a mustard seed, you will say to this mountain, 'Move from here to there,' and it will move; and nothing will be impossible for you."

MATTHEW 17:20

If our faith isn't rooted in the Bible, it will wither like a plant pulled out of the soil. Only a strong faith—a faith based on God's Word—will protect us from temptation and doubt.

Do you want your faith to grow? Then let the Bible begin to saturate your mind and soul. One of my most enduring memories of my mother is of her sitting quietly in her favorite chair, reading her well-worn Bible every day. This was her practice right up to the end of her life and was the reason she had such an unwavering faith. The Bible says, "faith comes from hearing the message, and the message is heard through the word about Christ" (Romans 10:17 NIV). Faith doesn't just happen; it grows when it is planted in the fertile soil of God's Word.

PEACE WITH GOD

Let the peace of God rule in your hearts.

COLOSSIANS 3:15

Science has confirmed what the Bible taught centuries ago: there is a close relationship between our minds and bodies. Proverbs puts it this way: "A cheerful heart is good medicine, but a crushed spirit dries up the bones" (Proverbs 17:22 NIV).

But there is also a close relationship between our mental and physical health and the health of our spiritual lives. Guilt, fear, jealousy, bitterness, futility, escapism—these and a host of other problems are spiritual ills brought about by the disease of sin. Like poison, they can sicken us in mind and body.

But when Christ comes into our lives, He removes our guilt and takes away our fears. He gives us love for others and a new purpose in life. His joy and peace neutralize sin's poison—and that promotes emotional and physical health. Does that mean our emotional and physical problems will vanish? Not necessarily. But like a spring of pure water, God's peace in our hearts brings cleansing and refreshment to our minds and bodies.

POWER IN GOD'S WORD

The word of God is living and powerful, and sharper
than any two-edged sword, piercing even to the division
of soul and spirit, and of joints and marrow, and is a
discerner of the thoughts and intents of the heart.

HEBREWS 4:12

There is power in the Word of God—the power to change our lives. "'Is not my word like fire,' declares the LORD, 'and like a hammer that breaks a rock in pieces?'" (Jeremiah 23:29 NIV).

God spoke—and the heavens were formed. God spoke—and the Red Sea parted so the Israelites could escape from slavery. God spoke—and Jesus Christ rose from the dead. God spoke—and Saul, the hate-filled persecutor, was converted and became Paul the apostle. Yes, there is power in the Word of God. When I quote the words of the Bible in my preaching, I know that the Holy Spirit will take those words and supernaturally use them to bring conviction and new life to others. I know, too, that when I prayerfully study the Bible on my own, God will use it to change me. He can do the same for you.

Infinite Grace

Grace and truth came through Jesus Christ.

John 1:17

The word *grace* means more than just God's kindness or gentleness toward us, or even His mercy. It means His undeserved favor. It means God owes nothing to us, and we deserve nothing from Him. When the Bible says "by grace you have been saved" (Ephesians 2:5), it means our salvation was totally unmerited. It came solely because of God's grace.

The motive of grace is the infinite, compassionate love of a merciful God, but the work of grace was Christ's death on the Cross. When I imagine Christ hanging from the Cross, the spikes in His hands, the crown of thorns on His brow, His blood draining from His body, the soldiers mocking Him—then I begin to see the depth of God's grace. Then I know that nothing can equal the infinite love of God for a sinful world.

But God's grace is also exhibited when we humbly bow before Christ in repentance and faith, for then we find forgiveness. Thank God for His grace, for without it we would have no hope!

The Practice of Prayer

"Whatever things you ask in prayer, believing, you will receive."
MATTHEW 21:22

I don't think I ever met a busier man than my father-in-law, Dr. L. Nelson Bell. Yet my most lasting memory of Dr. Bell is his commitment to prayer. Most mornings he would be up by four thirty or five o'clock, alone in his study reading his well-worn Bible and spending extended time in prayer. If anyone had an excuse to bypass this it was Dr. Bell—but he saw his time alone with God as the most important event of the day. He never drew attention to it (much less bragged about it), but occasionally he would quote the Psalmist's words: "O God, thou art my God; early will I seek thee: my soul thirsteth for thee" (Psalm 63:1 KJV).

Prayer for Dr. Bell wasn't a hurried sentence or two at the end of the day or a hasty afterthought when facing a crisis. Prayer for him was a constant, moment-by-moment practice that penetrated his whole life. Prayer for him was also a joyful experience, an opportunity to come daily into God's presence. So should it be for us.

THE FUTURE LIFE

As for man, his days are like grass;
As a flower of the field, so he flourishes.

PSALM 103:15

The Bible reminds us that our days are as grass. For a brief time we flourish, but soon we wither and die. Yet the minutes of our lives can be flecked with the gold of eternity. Instead of wasting them—as we so easily do—God exhorts us to redeem the time.

But our lives are also immortal. God made us different from the other creatures. He made us in His own image, a living soul. Don't let anyone tell you that we are simply a higher species of animal. If you believe that, you will begin to act like one. No! You are far greater.

One thousand years from this day you will be more alive than you are at this moment. The Bible teaches that life does not end at the cemetery. There is a future life with God for those who put their trust in His Son, Jesus Christ. Make sure of your relationship to Christ, and then ask God to help you live each day for His glory.

God's Holiness

"Holy, holy, holy is the LORD of hosts;
The whole earth is full of His glory!"

ISAIAH 6:3

The Bible teaches that God is absolutely holy and pure. From Genesis to Revelation, God reveals Himself as so holy He cannot even look on sin. Christ cried from the Cross, "My God, My God, why have You forsaken Me?" (Mark 15:34). What a horrible moment, as the blackness of human sin—now laid upon Christ—caused the Father to turn away in disgust. In that moment Jesus endured the ultimate punishment for our sins—the punishment of being banished from the presence of His Father on our behalf.

If you were asked to list the things you are thankful for, what would you include? Perhaps your family, health, friends, church—and those wouldn't be wrong. We should be grateful for every gift God gives us. But the greatest gift of all is the gift of His Son, who endured the penalty we deserved for our sin, so we could be reconciled to a holy God. Never take that gift for granted! "Thanks be to God for His indescribable gift!" (2 Corinthians 9:15).

SHARING DEEPLY

This is the confidence that we have in Him, that if we ask anything according to His will, He hears us.

1 JOHN 5:14

Prayer shouldn't be a burden but a privilege—a privilege God has graciously given us because He wants our fellowship. Remember that Jesus Christ died to destroy the barrier of sin that separates us from God, and when we give our lives to Him, we have a personal relationship with God. In fact, we have access to God in prayer only because of what Christ did for us by His death and resurrection.

But central to any relationship is communication. It's true on a human level; what kind of relationship do two people have who never talk with each other? In a far greater way, our relationship with God involves communication—not just an occasional brief chat, but a deep sharing of ourselves and our concerns with God.

CHRIST'S PROMISE

"I am with you always, to the very end of the age."

MATTHEW 28:20 NIV

These words are Christ's promise to all His disciples, and it is a promise that is marvelously inclusive. No situation is excluded; no challenge is omitted. Dr. Handley Moule, the noted Greek scholar and Anglican Bishop of Durham (England) in another generation, maintained that the word *always* could be paraphrased to mean, "I am with you all the days, all day long." That means we can count on Christ's presence not only every day, but also every moment of every day. Of the fact of His presence there can be no doubt, for His Word cannot fail.

What we need is to cultivate the sense of His presence, every day, every hour, every moment. This happens as we speak to Him in worship and prayer, and listen to Him speak to us through His Word, the Bible.

Everything We Need

I will pray with the spirit, and I will also pray with the understanding.

1 Corinthians 14:15

Why do we need to pray? The reason is because the Christian life is a journey, and we need God's strength and guidance along the way. One of the major ways He supplies these is through prayer. God doesn't leave us to our own resources! Instead, He "has given us *everything we need* for a godly life through our knowledge of him who called us by his own glory and goodness" (2 Peter 1:3 NIV, emphasis added). Prayer is part of the "everything we need" God has given us.

A prayerless Christian is a powerless Christian. A prayerless Christian is also a contradiction, because we should yearn for fellowship with the One who redeemed us. Throughout both the Bible and the history of the Church, those who made the greatest impact for God were those who prayed the most.

Accept God's Freedom

Draw near to God and He will draw near to you.

JAMES 4:8

One day a little child was playing with a valuable vase. He put his hand into it and could not take it out. His father, too, tried his best to get the little boy's hand out, but all in vain. They were thinking of breaking the vase when the father said, "Now, my son, make one more try. Open your hand and hold your fingers out straight as you see me doing and then pull."

To the father's astonishment the little fellow said, "Oh no, Daddy. I couldn't put my fingers out like that because if I did I would drop my penny." Smile if you will—but thousands of us are like that little boy, so busy holding on to the world's worthless trifles that we cannot accept God's freedom. What "trifle" is keeping you from God? A sin you won't let go of? An unworthy goal you are determined to reach? A dishonorable relationship you won't give up? I beg you to drop that trifle in your heart. Surrender! Let go and let God have His way in your life.

GUIDED *by* GOD'S LOVE

*We have known and
believed the love that God
has for us.*

1 JOHN 4:16

White as Snow

Wash me, and I shall be whiter than snow.

PSALM 51:7

Snow is so white that we can see almost anything that is dropped on it, even at great distances. We can take the whitest object we can find, like newly washed clothing, but when we place it next to snow, it may look dirty by comparison. Our lives are like that. At times, we may think of ourselves as morally good and decent; we are content that "we are not like other men." But compared to God's purity, we are defiled and filthy.

In spite of our sins and uncleanness, God still loves us. And because He loves us, He decided to provide for us a purity we could never attain on our own. That is why He gave His Son, Jesus Christ, to die for us on the Cross. Only when our sins have been washed in the blood of Jesus Christ will we appear as white as snow in the eyes of God.

Thank God today that you are now "whiter than snow," because "you were washed . . . in the name of the Lord Jesus and by the Spirit of our God" (1 Corinthians 6:11).

GOD WANTS OUR FELLOWSHIP

Come near to God and he will come near to you.

JAMES 4:8 NIV

What a blessed promise and provision this is! It means each of us can come close to God, with the assurance He will come close to us—so close that we become conscious of His presence. This is the greatest experience we can know.

But for most of us this isn't easy. Life presents us with too many distractions, and the last thing we have time for is to be alone with God. Children, work, television, the Internet, even church activities drain away our time. Maybe you will have to readjust your priorities. Maybe you will have to say no to certain activities or demands. Whatever it takes, make time to be alone with God.

Remember: He wants your fellowship, and He has done everything possible to make it a reality. He has forgiven your sins, at the cost of His own dear Son. He has given you His Word and the priceless privilege of prayer and worship. He will come near to you, if you will come near to Him.

THE TRIUMPHS OF GRACE

"I, even I, am He who blots out your transgressions . . ."

ISAIAH 43:25

When Charles Wesley experienced the joy of divine for-giveness, he told a Moravian friend of his new sense of pardon, and added, "I suppose I had better keep silent about it."

"Oh, no, my brother," came the reply. "If you had a thou-sand tongues, you should go and use them all for Jesus."

Charles Wesley went home and wrote the great hymn:

"Oh for a thousand tongues to sing
My great Redeemer's praise,
The glories of my God and King,
The triumphs of His grace!"

To a burdened, benighted world, crushed under the weight of its own wickedness, God says, "I, even I, am He who blots out your transgressions" (Isaiah 43:25). This is glorious news, and it applies to all people every-where—including you. Have you received God's gift of forgiveness? If you have, thank Him for it—and if not, by faith invite Christ into your life today.

THE RIGHT QUESTION

"They seek Me daily,
And delight to know My ways."

ISAIAH 58:2

Life isn't always fair, nor is it always the way we wish it were. Disappointment, tragedy, grief, failure, disability, illness, injustice, rejection, suffering, grief—these will come our way, sometimes at the most unexpected times or in the most unexpected ways.

When they do, it's natural to ask "Why, Lord? Why did You let this happen to me?" It's not wrong to ask this; God may even answer our cry (or at least give us a hint) because He has lessons to teach us through this experience.

But the most important question we should ask when life turns against us isn't "Why?" but "What?" "What do You want me to do, Lord? What should my reaction be to this situation? What response do You want me to take?"

The Light of God's Love

O Lord my God, You are very great....
You who laid the foundations of the earth.

Psalm 104:1, 5

God's love did not begin at Calvary. Before the morning stars sang together, before the world was baptized with the first light, before the first blades of tender grass peeped out, God was love. Turn back to the unwritten pages of countless eons before God spoke this present earth into existence, when the earth was "without form and void" and the deep, silent darkness of space stood in stark contrast to the brilliance of God's glory and His cherubim and seraphim.

Even then, God was love. Before the worlds were created, He knew all about us and the need we would have someday for Christ to die for us. So in His love "he chose us in him before the creation of the world" (Ephesians 1:4 NIV). God does not change—and neither does His love. He loved you before you were born . . . He loves you now . . . and He will love you forever. Will you love Him in return?

Strong Foundations

"Is there a God besides Me?
Indeed there is no other Rock;
I know not one."

ISAIAH 44:8

The time to prepare for life's disappointments and hurts is in advance, before they come crashing down upon us. Now is the time to build spiritual foundations that won't collapse under the weight of life's reverses.

Some time ago the remnants of a powerful hurricane tore down numerous trees around our home and caused several landslides. But the house itself was untouched because, when it was being built, an architect friend advised us to set it on steel pilings driven down to solid rock, which we did.

How strong is the foundation of your life? And what are you doing to make it stronger? A house's foundation isn't built in a day, nor are our spiritual foundations. Make it your goal to build strong foundations for your life—foundations constructed from prayer and the truths of God's Word.

The Good Shepherd

One of the figures of speech Jesus applied to Himself was that of a shepherd. He said, "I am the good shepherd. The good shepherd lays down his life for the sheep. The hired hand is not the shepherd and does not own the sheep. . . . I know my sheep and my sheep know me" (John 10:11–12, 14 NIV). Note four things about Jesus, the Good Shepherd. He owns the sheep; they belong to Him. Next, He guards the sheep; He never abandons them when danger approaches. Also, He knows the sheep; He calls them by name and they follow Him. Finally, He lays down His life for the sheep; their salvation is His primary concern.

The Bible says, "We are His people and the sheep of His pasture" (Psalm 100:3). Because we belong to Christ, we can be secure and at rest.

The Depth of God's Love

He shall cover you with His feathers,
And under His wings you shall take refuge.

Psalm 91:4

I still recall how stunned I felt when news came that one of my closest friends in high school had been shot down in a fighter plane over Germany. Recovering from grief, I've come to realize, isn't a single event but a process. Just as our bodies heal only gradually after major surgery, so too do our hearts after the death of someone we loved.

The Psalmist wrote, "Cast your burden on the Lord, and He shall sustain you" (Psalm 55:22). Notice that he didn't say, "Cast some of your burden on the Lord." Instead, God wants us to cast all our burdens on Him—including our burden of grief. Your grief over the death of someone you loved may be the biggest burden you will ever carry. Why carry it alone? Why not turn it over to God?

We will only do this when we realize two great truths: the depth of our weakness and the depth of God's love. Don't try to carry your grief alone! Instead, turn to your loving Heavenly Father and ask Him to lift it from your shoulders—and slowly but surely He will.

God's Hand of Blessing

Every good gift and every perfect gift is from above.

JAMES 1:17

In the midst of the Lord's Prayer are these familiar words: "Give us this day our daily bread" (Matthew 6:11). They remind us that we are dependent on God for everything, and He is the giver of every blessing. "Every good gift and every perfect gift is from above, and comes down from the Father of lights" (James 1:17).

Some people say, "Why should I pray for my daily bread? I can take care of my own needs!" But listen: if it weren't for God's love and grace, you wouldn't have anything. We need to pray this prayer every day because we need to be reminded to trust God in everything.

This prayer reminds us also of Jesus' words: "I am the bread of life. He who comes to Me shall never hunger" (John 6:35). Thank God for all His gifts—especially Christ, the greatest gift of all.

GOD'S PERFECT WILL

"My grace is sufficient for you, for My strength is made perfect in weakness."

2 CORINTHIANS 12:9

When we're healthy, we easily become busy and preoccupied with the present—and end up forgetting God. But when accident or illness set us aside, we have time to reflect on what's really important. Most of all, we have time to examine our relationship with Christ and recommit ourselves and our futures into His loving hands. Throughout the ages, suffering Christians have found that the Bible's promise is true: "The LORD is near to all who call on him, to all who call on him in truth" (Psalm 145:18 NIV). The Bible also says, "The eternal God is your refuge, and underneath are the everlasting arms" (Deuteronomy 33:27 NIV).

When suffering comes, learn to trust each day into God's hands and take it as a gift from Him. In addition, even if you can't concentrate very well, let your lips be filled with prayer and praise. Yes, pray for healing; God is sovereign, and He is able to intervene. But most of all pray for His will to be done in your life—for His will is perfect.

THE KNOWLEDGE OF GOD

Oh, the depth of the riches both of the wisdom and knowledge of God!

ROMANS 11:33

We have always tried to understand the world around us; it is one of the things that sets us apart from the animals. Some of the mysteries of the past have been fathomed by science. Others still puzzle us. This fact remains: all of the garnered wisdom of the ages is only a scratch on the surface of humanity's search for the knowledge of the universe.

This inability to comprehend fully the mysteries of God's creation does not in any way cast doubt on the Christian faith. On the contrary, it enhances our belief. We do not understand the intricate patterns of the stars in their courses, but we know that He who created them does, and that just as surely as He guides them, He is charting a safe course for us.

The next time you look into the heavens at night, remember the words of the Psalmist: "The heavens declare the glory of God" (Psalm 19:1).

The Hallmark of Love

Beloved, let us love one another, for love is of God; and everyone who loves is born of God and knows God. He who does not love does not know God, for God is love.

1 John 4:7–8

What the original Greek language of the New Testament called "agape" love is selfless love—love that extends even to those who aren't lovable or even worthy of love. The Bible says this is the kind of love God has for us—and is the kind of love we should have for others.

The love God wants us to have isn't just an emotion, but a conscious act of the will—a deliberate decision on our part to put others ahead of ourselves. The Bible says, "Let each of you look out not only for his own interests, but also for the interests of others" (Philippians 2:4). This is the kind of love God has for us—a love so deep that it caused Christ to leave Heaven's glory and die on the cross for us. The opposite of agape love is selfishness, but when Christ's love fills our hearts, it puts selfishness on the run.

What is God's priority for you? God's priority is that His love would become the hallmark of your life—and the reason is because it was the hallmark of Christ's life.

GOD CONTROLS THE CLOCK

There is laid up for me the crown of righteousness.

2 TIMOTHY 4:8

Many people are asking, "Where is history heading?" A careful student of the Bible will see that God controls the clock of destiny. Amidst the world's confusion, God's omnipotent hand moves, working out His unchanging plan and purpose.

Not that we always see His hand at work. As the old English hymn writer William Cowper put it, "God moves in a mysterious way, His wonders to perform." God is not absent. By His providence He sustains us, and behind the scenes He is working to bring about His divine purpose.

What is that purpose? Paul recorded it this way: "That . . . He might gather together in one all things in Christ, both which are in heaven and which are on earth" (Ephesians 1:10). Someday Satan's rule will be ended, and Christ will reign as Lord over all creation. Someday all the sin and rebellion of this corrupted universe will be destroyed, and Christ's kingdom of righteousness and peace will rule forever. Don't be discouraged by what you see in the headlines every day. God is at work, and someday Christ will rule.

FREELY FORGIVE

"Judge not, and you shall not be judged. Condemn not, and you shall not be condemned. Forgive, and you will be forgiven."

LUKE 6:37

Almost every week someone writes me saying something like this: "I can't forgive. You don't know how deeply I've been hurt." Perhaps this echoes your own thoughts. But nothing releases us from the past or opens the door to reconciliation as completely as forgiveness. Even if the other person refuses to admit any fault or scorns our forgiveness, that mustn't hold us back.

The Bible is clear: "Bear with each other and forgive one another if any of you has a grievance against someone else. Forgive as the Lord forgave you" (Colossians 3:13 NIV).

Did you notice that last phrase? God forgave us freely and fully in Christ, and that's how we are to forgive others: freely and fully. It may be the hardest thing you ever do, but with God's help you can—and you must.

The Hope of the Centuries

*It is good that one should hope and wait quietly
for the salvation of the Lord.*

LAMENTATIONS 3:26

The promised coming of Christ has been the great hope of believers down through the centuries. The ancient Nicene Creed affirms, "He shall come again with glory." Charles Wesley wrote 7,000 hymns; 5,000 mention the coming of Christ. As the Archbishop of Canterbury crowned Queen Elizabeth II, he stated, "I give thee, O Sovereign Lady, this crown to wear until He who reserves the right to wear it shall return."

But until that time, our world remains in the grip of violence and despair. One noted columnist summed it up this way: "For us all, the world is disorderly and dangerous; ungoverned, and apparently ungovernable."

Someday, however, the King will return. Someday the heavens will shout, "The kingdoms of this world have become the kingdoms of our Lord and of His Christ, and He shall reign forever and ever!" (Revelation 11:15). Christ alone is the answer to the burdens of our hearts and the hopelessness of our world.

The Gift of Each Day

One thing I have desired of the LORD,
That will I seek:
That I may dwell in the house of the LORD
All the days of my life,
To behold the beauty of the LORD,
And to inquire in His temple.

PSALM 27:4

Each day is a gift from God. It is another opportunity God has given you to serve Him. Time isn't inexhaustible, nor can we assume we'll always have more; someday our time on earth will end. The Psalmist said, "My times are in your hands" (Psalm 31:15 NIV). The first thing we should do when we awake is thank God for the gift of another day. The second is to commit our time to God.

God gave it to us for a reason: not to be wasted or mishandled, but to be used for His glory. We are accountable to Him for the way we use our time, and once a minute passes it can never be reclaimed. The Bible says, we always should be "redeeming the time, because the days are evil" (Ephesians 5:16).

Serving Eternally

You have a better and an enduring possession for yourselves in heaven.

HEBREWS 10:34

Some people think Heaven will be dull and boring, but nothing could be further from the truth. The Father's house will be a happy home because there will be work to do there. John wrote in Revelation 22:3, "His servants shall serve Him." Each one will be given exactly the task that suits his powers, his tastes, and his abilities. And the Father's house will be a happy home because friends will be there. Have you ever been to a strange place and had the joy of seeing a familiar face? Not one of us who enters the Father's house will feel lonely or strange, for we who have put our trust in Christ are part of His family, sharing Heaven's joys forever with all our brothers and sisters in Christ.

Alexander MacLaren described Heaven this way: "The joys of heaven are not the joys of passive contemplation, of dreamy remembrance . . . but they are described thus, 'They rest not night nor day,' and 'His servants serve Him and see His face.'" In the midst of earth's turmoil, keep your eyes on Heaven!

From God's Hand

Let the beauty of the LORD our God be upon us,
And establish the work of our hands for us;
Yes, establish the work of our hands.

PSALM 90:17

Instead of seeing your job as a burden, see it as a responsibility given to you by God. No matter what your work is, if it is legitimate, then it has dignity, for it came from God. Our work may seem burdensome and meaningless, but once we realize God gave it to us, our attitude will change. The writer of Ecclesiastes discovered this truth: "A person can do nothing better than . . . find satisfaction in their own toil. This too, I see, is from the hand of God" (Ecclesiastes 2:24 NIV).

We often speak of someone being "called" by God to the ministry or mission field, but if you know Christ and are in His will, you also have been called—to your vocation. (In fact, the word "vocation" comes from a Latin word meaning "to be called.") Does this mean our work will never be dull or hard or tiring? No, of course not. But when we see our work as something God gave us, even the most routine tasks take on significance.

The Greatest Security

He who dwells in the secret place of the Most High
Shall abide under the shadow of the Almighty.

PSALM 91:1

Someone has said that the only certainty in life is uncertainty—and it is true. Governments collapse, stock markets plummet, wars destroy, disasters strike, relationships end. As the writer of Hebrews put it, "Here we have no continuing city" (Hebrews 13:14). Yet deep in the human heart is a yearning for security—a yearning that will not go away. We know we need a solid foundation to life, a foundation that cannot be shaken. Where will it be found?

Only God never changes. His love does not change, and neither do His promises. That is why we can look to Him for the security and stability we all seek. King David knew the secret: "He who dwells in the secret place of the Most High shall abide under the shadow of the Almighty" (Psalm 91:1).

Salvation is not an occasional, vague feeling of God's presence. It is actually dwelling with God, secure in His presence forever. Is your security in Christ?

GOD KNOWS WHAT IS BEST

Search me, O God, and know my heart . . .
And lead me in the way everlasting.

PSALM 139:23–24

Does God really care about the decisions we make? Does God have a plan for our lives—a plan we can actually know? Or does He expect us to make all our decisions on our own?

The Bible's answer is clear: God knows all about us, and He knows what is best for us. He sees the dangers we face, and He also knows the joys we could experience. But God not only knows what is best for us, He also wants what is best for us. The reason is simple: He loves us.

One of the most important truths I can say about God's will is this: God's will comes from God's love. If God didn't love us, He wouldn't care which way we went when we face a decision. But He does love us—and that makes all the difference. Because He loves us, we can confidently seek His will, knowing it is always best for us—always.

WALK WITH GOD

My eyes shall be on the faithful of the land,
That they may dwell with me.

PSALM 101:6

Walk with God as Noah did; when the flood came, Noah was saved amidst the scorn and rejection of his neighbors. Walk with God as Moses did in the solitude of the desert; when the hour of judgment fell upon Egypt, Moses was prepared to lead his people to victory. Walk with God as David did as a shepherd boy; when he was called to rule his people he was prepared for the task of kingship. Walk with God as Daniel and his three young friends did in the palace of Babylon's king; when the fiery furnace and the lion's den came, God was beside them and delivered them.

No, God didn't always deliver His saints from adversity or even death, nor does He today. But because they had learned to trust Him in the light, they were prepared to follow Him in the darkness. God has not promised to deliver us from trouble, but He has promised to go with us through the trouble.

"Yea, though I walk through the valley of the shadow of death, I will fear no evil; for You are with me" (Psalm 23:4).

VICTORY IN JESUS

Thanks be to God, who gives us the victory through our Lord Jesus Christ.

1 CORINTHIANS 15:57 NRSV

Joseph Haydn, the great musician, was once asked why his church music was so cheerful. He replied, "When I think upon God, my heart is so full of joy that the notes dance and leap, as it were, from my pen, and since God has given me a cheerful heart, it will be pardoned me that I serve Him with a cheerful spirit."

Haydn had discovered the secret to lasting joy: "I think upon God." Looking at our circumstances won't bring us lasting joy. It may even make us depressed or angry. But when we "think on God"—when we turn our minds and hearts to His power and His love for us, we can't help but be joyful. Paul said, "Set your mind on things above, not on things on the earth" (Colossians 3:2). Discouragement flees in the face of joy.

Every day brings battles and temptations. But the strength we need for conquering them comes from Christ. We can do like the little girl who said that when the devil came knocking with a temptation, she just sent Jesus to the door!

STRENGTHENED
by GOD'S LOVE

*Neither death nor
life, nor angels nor
principalities . . . shall be
able to separate us from
the love of God.*

ROMANS 8:38–39

GROWING STRONGER

But grow in the grace and knowledge of our Lord and Savior Jesus Christ.

2 PETER 3:18

Many years ago, engineers made plans to construct a suspension bridge over a deep river gorge. The biggest problem was how to get the heavy steel cables from one side of the gorge to the other. Helicopters hadn't been invented, and the rock-strewn river below made it too dangerous to transfer the cables by boat.

The solution? One day the engineers flew a kite over the gorge. As it hovered over the opposite shore, they deliberately grounded it—which meant the two sides of the river were now linked by a thin kite string. They then tied a slightly heavier string to one end of the kite string and carefully hauled it across to the other side. They repeated this process several more times, graduating on to stronger ropes, until eventually they were able to pull the heavy steel cables across the gorge and construct the bridge.

Spiritual growth is like the construction of that bridge. Just as the link between the gorge gradually grew stronger, so God's will is for our faith to grow stronger and stronger.

GOD PROMISES PROTECTION

"I will never leave you nor forsake you."

HEBREWS 13:5

Never doubt that you are in the midst of a battle—a spiritual battle with Satan, who will do everything he can to discourage and defeat you. Never underestimate his determination or misunderstand his intentions. God wants to teach us how to defend ourselves against sin and Satan. Satan, the ultimate bully, attacks us at our weakest points and wants to defeat us so that we will not be effective for God.

God offers spiritual "training" to build us up inside in much the same way that physical exercise can build us up on the outside. He has also provided all the resources we need to defend ourselves and keep Satan at bay. These include the Bible, prayer, faith, righteous living, and the Holy Spirit within us.

But, like physical training, we must be diligent in their application. God has not promised to shield us from trouble, but He has promised to protect us in the midst of trouble. Most of all, never forget that because of Christ's death and resurrection, Satan is already a defeated foe—and someday the war will be over.

Refined and Purified

When He has tested me, I shall come forth as gold.

Job 23:10

Affliction can be a means of refining and of purification. Just as ore must pass through the refiner's furnace before it can yield up its gold, so our lives must sometimes pass through God's furnace of affliction before they can bring forth something beautiful and useful to Him. We might never have had the songs of Fanny Crosby had she not been afflicted with blindness. George Matheson would never have given the world his immortal song, "O Love That Wilt Not Let Me Go," had it not been for the pain of personal tragedy and heartache. The "Hallelujah Chorus" was written by Handel when he was poverty-stricken and suffering from a paralyzed right side and right arm.

Affliction can also make us stronger in our faith and develop our confidence in God's watch care over us. It may also drive us back to the right path when we have wandered. David said, "Before I was afflicted I went astray, but now I keep Your word" (Psalm 119:67). Whatever the reason, if God sends affliction your way, take it in faith as a blessing not a curse.

WHY DID HE DIE?

The message of the cross . . . is the power of God.

1 CORINTHIANS 1:18

We can never grasp the horror of human sin until we realize it caused the Son of God to be crucified. Not Pilate, not Judas, not the mob—but sin. The ravages of war and poverty, the wrenching pain of loneliness and rejection. The haunting cry of the orphan and widow, the dying gasps of the world's starving—these and a thousand other tragedies all bear witness to the fact that we live in a world poisoned by sin. And that is why Jesus died. The terrible, bitter cup of humanity's sin sent Him to the Cross. Jesus prayed in those last hours, "O, My Father, if it is possible, let this cup pass from Me; nevertheless, not as I will, but as You will" (Matthew 26:39). There was no other way. Why did He drink that awful cup? So you and I would not have to.

Sin is the second most powerful force in the universe, for it sent Jesus to the Cross. Only one force is greater—the love of God.

PROMISE OF FORGIVENESS

Create in me a clean heart, O God,
And renew a steadfast spirit within me.

PSALM 51:10

Sin breaks our fellowship with God—but it doesn't end our relationship. We are still His children, even when we disobey. We feel guilty and ashamed, and sometimes we simply want to hide. But God still loves us, and He wants to forgive us and welcome us back! When you fail, repent and claim God's promise of forgiveness and restoration.

The Bible promises, "If we confess our sins, he is faithful and just and will forgive us our sins and purify us from all unrighteousness" (1 John 1:9 NIV). This is God's promise to you. Believe it!

The only sin God cannot forgive is the sin of refusing His forgiveness. When you sin, don't excuse it, or ignore it, or blame it on someone else. Admit it . . . repent of it . . . and then rejoice that God has fully forgiven you.

God Is Our Strength

The LORD is my light and my salvation;
Whom shall I fear?

PSALM 27:1

It is a fact that the Lord is my light and my salvation. So why should I be afraid? Since the Lord fears nothing, why should we fear?

The Scripture also declares that God is a "very present help in trouble" (Psalm 46:1). If we can't trust the all-powerful, all-knowing, all-loving God of the universe to help us, where can we turn? But we can trust Him! God is able, indeed He is anxious, to deliver us from all sorts of trouble. He wants to give us strength to overcome the temptation to sin that separates Him from those He loves. He wants to give us the courage to confront our problems (instead of avoiding them or denying them), and then to find the practical wisdom and help we need to deal with them.

What do you fear today? Failure? Rejection? An illness or physical danger? The uncertainty of the future? Whatever it is, ask God to help you turn it over to Him. "The LORD is my light and my salvation; whom shall I fear?" (Psalm 27:1).

Free from Sin

Keep your heart with all diligence,
For out of it spring the issues of life.

Proverbs 4:23

When King David refused to confess his adultery with Bathsheba and suppressed his feelings of guilt, he paid a price both spiritually and physically: "When I kept silent, my bones wasted away . . . my strength was sapped" (Psalm 32:3–4 NIV). Only when he faced his sin and sought God's forgiveness did his health return. The Bible says, "A cheerful heart is good medicine, but a crushed spirit dries up the bones" (Proverbs 17:22 NIV).

Sin, like a deadly cancer, has invaded every area of our lives: our bodies, our minds, our emotions, our wills—everything. Don't take sin lightly! But Jesus Christ came to conquer sin. He came not only to forgive us, but also came to free us from sin's power and transform us by His Spirit. The Bible says, "Once you were alienated from God. . . . But now he has reconciled you . . . to present you holy in his sight, without blemish and free from accusation" (Colossians 1:21–22 NIV).

Holy, without blemish, free from accusation—this is God's purpose for you every day.

PEACE, PERFECT PEACE

I will give you assured peace in this place.

JEREMIAH 14:13

"Worry," says Vance Havner, "is like sitting in a rocking chair. It will give you something to do, but it won't get you anywhere." Worry and anxiety have hounded the human race since the beginning of time, and modern man with all his innovations has not found the cure for the plague of worry. What is the answer? Imagine in your mind a ferocious ocean storm beating against a rocky shore. The lightning flashes, the thunder roars, the waves lash the rocks. But then imagine that you see a crevice in the rocky cliff—and inside is a little bird, its head serenely tucked under its wing, fast asleep. It knows the rock will protect it, and thus it sleeps in peace.

God promised Moses, "I will put you in the cleft of the rock, and will cover you with My hand" (Exodus 33:22). That is God's promise to us. Christ is our Rock, and we are secure in His hands forever. The storm rages, but our hearts are at rest.

God Is in Control

The Lord is on my side;
I will not fear.

Psalm 118:6

What is the opposite of fear? For the Christian there can be only one answer: the opposite of fear is trust—trust in God and His unchanging love. Once we realize God is in control and He holds us in His loving hands, we can meet life's dangers and uncertainties with confidence. After all, if we can trust God for our eternal salvation, can't we also trust Him for our lives right now?

Let's be honest, however. It's hard to trust God when danger threatens or everything seems to be collapsing around us. Fear comes much easier to us than faith. But never forget: fear can banish faith, but faith can banish fear. Faith isn't pretending our problems don't exist, nor is it simply blind optimism. Faith points us beyond our problems to the hope we have in Christ. True faith involves trust—trust in what Christ has done for us, and trust in God's goodness and mercy.

Risen and Returning

"This same Jesus . . . will so come in like manner as you saw Him go."

ACTS 1:11

The resurrection of Jesus Christ is the key to God's plan for the future. Unless Christ was raised from the dead, there can be no future kingdom and no returning King. Unless Christ was raised from the dead, sin and death still reign, and God's plan of redemption remains unfulfilled. But Christ has been raised!

As the disciples stood watching after Jesus ascended into the heavens, the angels assured them that the risen Christ would someday be the returning Christ. "Men of Galilee, why do you stand gazing up into heaven? This same Jesus, who was taken up from you into heaven, will so come in like manner as you saw Him go into heaven" (Acts 1:11).

Just as surely as Christ rose from the dead, so He will return and take us to Him. Every promise—without exception—will be fulfilled.

The Promises of God

"There has not failed one word of all His good promise."

1 Kings 8:56

In the Bible God has given us "very great and precious promises" (2 Peter 1:4 NIV)—and every one of them reminds us that we can trust our lives into His hands. You can trust God's promises, for He cannot lie! God's promises in the Old Testament are just as applicable and relevant to us today as those in the New Testament, and both Testaments contain God's principles for life. Fear vanishes when it is exposed to the promises of God's Word.

What are those promises? One is that God is with you, no matter how difficult or confusing life becomes. He says, "Never will I leave you; never will I forsake you" (Hebrews 13:5 NIV). Jesus declared, "Surely I am with you always, to the very end of the age" (Matthew 28:20 NIV). You are never alone if you know Christ—never. I have never forgotten the familiar words from Psalm 23 my mother taught me as a child: "Yea, though I walk through the valley of the shadow of death, I will fear no evil: for thou art with me; thy rod and thy staff they comfort me" (Psalm 23:4 KJV). Saturate your mind and heart with the promises of God's Word.

Perfect in Weakness

When I am weak, then I am strong.

2 Corinthians 12:10

God's idea of strength and man's idea of strength are opposite one another. The Lord told Paul, "My strength is made perfect in weakness" (2 Corinthians 12:9). Having learned this lesson, Paul could then say, "When I am weak, then I am strong" (2 Corinthians 12:10). A paradox? Not really. Only when Paul admitted his own weakness and was willing to get out of the way, could God take over and work.

If we try to do God's will in our own strength, then we can take the credit for whatever gets accomplished. But that isn't God's way! When we let His strength work through us, then He alone will get the glory—and that is as it should be.

In the Old Testament, God repeatedly told the leaders of Israel to reduce the size of their armies, or He announced in advance how their victory would be won. Why? So they would place their trust in Him and not in their own strength. As someone has said, "God's work, done in God's way, will never lack for God's provision."

Our Faithful God

Rest in the LORD, and wait patiently for Him.

PSALM 37:7

One of the most frequent questions people ask me concerns unanswered prayer. "God must be deaf," someone bluntly wrote me. "My prayers never get above the ceiling," another wrote. But God knows what is best for us, and we need to learn to trust Him for the outcome. Sometimes God answers "Yes" when we ask Him for something. But sometimes His answer is "Not yet," or even "No." And sometimes His answer is simply "Trust me, even if you don't understand."

Ruth's father, Dr. Bell, always kept a list of people for whom he was praying. After his death, Ruth found one of his prayer lists ("Mostly illegible," she commented. "You know how doctors write!"). On it was a specific concern about one of our children. Not until five years after his death was that prayer answered—a vivid reminder of God's faithfulness in answering prayer according to His timetable, not ours.

REDEEMED BY LOVE

You were redeemed . . . with the precious blood of Christ.
1 PETER 1:18–19 NIV

The word *redeem* means to "buy back"—to recover by paying a price. The word *redeemed* can be illustrated from the ancient world by the position of a slave who had been captured in battle or enticed into serving one who was not his legal master. His real master, however, intent on recovering his slave's service and love, would buy him back—redeem him from the enemy—at great personal cost.

That is what God did for us. Captured by Satan and enticed into his service, we were slaves of sin, without any hope of deliverance. But God still loved us, and He was determined to restore us to His household. By His death on the Cross, Jesus paid the price for our deliverance, a price far greater than our true value. He did it solely because He loved us. Now we have been redeemed!

Fear Not

If any of you lacks wisdom, let him ask of God, who gives to all liberally and without reproach, and it will be given to him.

James 1:5

The Bible's answer to worry couldn't be clearer: "Do not be anxious about anything, but in every situation, by prayer and petition, with thanksgiving, present your requests to God." Then comes God's promise: "And the peace of God, which transcends all understanding, will guard your hearts and your minds in Christ Jesus" (Philippians 4:6–7 NIV).

How should you pray? Pray, first of all, for strength in the face of whatever you fear, for God helps us hold on in the midst of life's storms. Pray also for wisdom to deal with whatever is worrying you; some practical steps may change the situation.

Pray as well that God will act to change your circumstances, according to His will. He doesn't always do what we want Him to—but He knows what's best for us, and He can be trusted. God is sovereign, and no situation is beyond His control. Over her desk my wife has these words: "Fear not the future; God is already there."

Living a Peaceable Life

Lead a quiet and peaceable life in all godliness and reverence.

1 Timothy 2:2

As Christians we aren't to isolate ourselves from the world in which we live. We are part of society, and we share in its difficulties, problems, and hopes. The Bible has much to say about our social responsibility. The Old Testament prophets condemned those who ignored the poor and exploited the weak. As Christians, we know human society is affected by sin, and any effort to improve society will always be incomplete and imperfect. We will never build a Utopia on earth.

But we must do all we can to alleviate suffering and to strike at the root causes of injustice, racial prejudice, hunger, and violence. We are to work for a peaceable life and human dignity for others. Why? Because God loves this suffering world. Jesus saw the crowds and "was moved with compassion" (Matthew 9:36).

Christ is concerned about the whole person—including the society in which that person lives. Do we share His concern?

REACH FOR HIS HAND

*The Lord, He is the One who goes before you. He will
be with you.*

DEUTERONOMY 31:8

Once many years ago, when I was going through a dark period, I prayed and prayed, but the heavens seemed to be brass. I felt as though God had disappeared and that I was alone with my trial and burden. It was a dark night for my soul.

I wrote my mother about the experience and will never forget her reply: "Son, there are many times when God withdraws to test your faith. He wants you to trust Him in the darkness. Now, Son, reach up by faith in the fog, and you will find that His hand will be there." In tears I knelt by my bed and experienced an overwhelming sense of God's presence.

Whether or not we feel God's presence when our way seems dark, by faith we know He is there. You can stake your life on His promise: "I will never leave you nor forsake you" (Hebrews 13:5).

Christ—Our Example

Being found in appearance as a man, He humbled Himself and became obedient to the point of death, even the death of the cross.

Philippians 2:8

One of the most memorable experiences of my life was the opportunity to visit a remote mountainous corner of India called Nagaland. Nagaland has one of the largest concentrations of Christians in India, and the occasion was the one hundredth anniversary of the coming of missionaries to that area. Tens of thousands came to the celebration—some walking for days over rough jungle trails. One hundred thousand people, we were told, would be gathering each morning for a Bible study, in addition to the evening evangelistic meetings.

When we arrived at Government House where we were to stay, a man unloaded our baggage from the car, then took our shoes to wipe the mud off them. I protested, saying we could do that, but he insisted. Only later did I discover that he would be leading the Bible study for those one hundred thousand people the next morning! Here was a man who truly exemplified the attitude of Christ by his humility and his willingness to serve others. I have never forgotten his example.

CHARACTER COUNTS

Be strong and of good courage; do not be afraid, nor be dismayed, for the LORD your God is with you wherever you go.

JOSHUA 1:9

Parts of the Great Wall date back before Christ, and it still stretches across hundreds of miles of rugged mountainous terrain. It was built for one purpose: to keep out barbarians bent on destroying Chinese civilization.

At first the Great Wall was a success; its height and well-guarded gates repelled every invasion. But eventually the enemy succeeded. How? The solution was simple: they found a gatekeeper of weak character and bribed him into leaving his gate unlocked.

Our lives are often like the Great Wall: strong and fortified at some points—but weak and vulnerable at others. And where will Satan attack? Not where he knows we are strong and he stands no chance of victory. A chain is only as strong as its weakest link, and so is our character. Know your weaknesses, and then with God's help turn them into strengths.

ALL-POWERFUL AND LOVING

How precious is Your lovingkindness, O God!
Therefore the children of men put their trust under the
shadow of Your wings.

PSALM 36:7

None of us will ever forget September 11, 2001. Within minutes our world changed forever. I was invited by the President to speak three days later at a special service of prayer and remembrance in Washington's National Cathedral. What could I say to bring comfort and hope to a nation in crisis?

"I have been asked hundreds of times in my life why God allows tragedy and suffering," I told the congregation that day. "I really do not know the answer totally, even to my own satisfaction. I have to accept, by faith, that God is sovereign, and He is a God of love and mercy and compassion in the midst of suffering."

Does that sound like a contradiction? Perhaps it does, at least to our limited minds. Yet both are true: evil is real—but so is God's power and love. And because He is all-powerful and loving, we can cling to Him in trust and faith, even when we don't understand.

God Understands Suffering

We are hard-pressed on every side, yet not crushed; we are perplexed, but not in despair.

2 Corinthians 4:8

Evil and suffering are real, whether we see them on our television screens or confront them in the privacy of our own lives. They aren't an illusion, nor are they simply an absence of good. None of us is immune from their grasp; suffering and tragedy touch us all, no matter who we are.

But God is also real! He is just as real as our pain and heartache—and even more so, for someday they will vanish, but He will still remain. In the midst of life's tragedies, He wants to assure us of His presence and love—even if we don't understand why He allowed them to happen. He knows what we are going through, for He experienced evil's fiercest assault when His beloved Son suffered the pangs of death and Hell. God understands our suffering, for Christ endured far greater suffering than we ever will. The Cross tells us that God understands our pain and confusion—but more than that, it tells us He loves us, and He will never abandon us.

SHAPED *by* GOD'S LOVE

God is love.

1 JOHN 4:8

GOD'S PERFECT PLAN

In all your ways acknowledge Him,
and He shall direct your paths.

PROVERBS 3:6

One of the happiest days of my life was when Ruth said she would be my wife. I could hardly contain my joy! But only a few years before I had faced one of the saddest days of my life, when another fine young woman with whom I thought I would be spending the rest of my life suddenly broke off our relationship. I was brokenhearted, convinced she must be making a mistake—but God knew better. Ruth was God's choice for me (just as I was God's choice for her), and I will always be grateful for His goodness in saving us for each other.

God has a personal, individual plan for each of us. It embraces the big things in life: who we will marry, what our career will be, where we will live, even when we will die. It also includes the details of our daily lives: decisions about our families, finances, leisure time, friendships, and countless other choices we make. No matter what decisions you are facing, seek His will—for His way is always best.

God's True Purposes

"Whatever you ask in My name, that I will do."

JOHN 14:13

Prayer links us with God's true purposes, for us and for the world. It not only brings the blessings of God's will to our own personal lives, it brings us the added blessing of being in step with God's plan. Prayer also—in ways we will never fully understand this side of eternity—makes us partners with God in what He is doing in the world. God works through our prayers!

The model prayer Jesus has given us concludes with, "Thine is the kingdom, and the power, and the glory for ever" (Matthew 6:13 KJV). Remember, too, that we must seek God's glory in our prayers and not just our own selfish desires. If we are to have our prayers answered, we must be willing to give God the glory when He acts—no matter what the result. Our Lord said to His disciples, "Whatever you ask in My name, that I will do, that the Father may be glorified in the Son" (John 14:13).

Shaped by God's Love

This is love, that we walk according to His commandments.

2 JOHN 6

God doesn't want to erase our personalities—although He does want to take the sharp edges off them! We are all different because God made us that way. Saul of Tarsus had what we today might call a "Type A" personality—hard-driving, determined, energetic, absolutely focused on his goal of destroying the Christian faith. But God intervened and replaced Saul's hatred of Christ with love. His basic personality didn't change, but God redirected his energies and used him instead (as the Apostle Paul) to advance the Gospel.

Paul's young companion Timothy, on the other hand, had a different personality—shy, sensitive, perhaps even a bit introverted. But God helped Timothy overcome his shyness so he could reach out to others, and God also used his sensitive nature to make him an effective and caring pastor. Thank God for making you the unique person you are, and ask Him to shape you and use you according to His will.

Joy on the Journey

The joy of the LORD is your strength.

NEHEMIAH 8:10

Some people have a warped idea of living the Christian life. Seeing talented, successful Christians, they attempt to imitate them. For them, the grass on the other side of the fence is always greener. But when they discover that their own gifts are different or their contributions are more modest (or even invisible), they collapse in discouragement and overlook genuine opportunities that are open to them. They have forgotten that they are here to serve Christ, not themselves.

Be like the apostle Paul and say, "None of these things move me" (Acts 20:24). Few men suffered as Paul did, yet he learned how to live above his circumstances—even in a prison cell. You can do the same. The key is to realize you are here to serve Christ, not yourself.

God does not promise us an easy life. He never promises that life will be perfect. He does not call His children to a playground, but to a battleground. In the midst of it all, when we serve Christ, we truly discover that "the joy of the Lord is [our] strength."

GUIDANCE FOR LIFE

I have not departed from Your judgments,
For You Yourself have taught me.

PSALM 119:102

When a soldier submits to the authority of his commanding officer, he obeys what that officer tells him to do. If a patient submits to a doctor's treatment, he or she does what the doctor says to do. If a football player submits to the direction of his coach, he does what the coach instructs him to do. And when we submit ourselves to the King of kings and the Lord of lords, we obey what He tells us to do, because we know His way is right.

God shows us His will first of all through His Word, the Bible. How many problems would we avoid if we knew God's Word and obeyed it? The Bible doesn't give us a rule for every conceivable situation—but it does cover far more than most of us realize. It also gives us principles by which we are to guide our lives. God's Word isn't to be debated or dissected; it is to be done.

A Home in Heaven

If I go and prepare a place for you, I will come again and receive you to Myself.

John 14:3

During Christ's ministry on earth He had no permanent home. He once said, "Foxes have dens and birds have nests, but the Son of Man has no place to lay his head" (Matthew 8:20 NIV).

What a contrast to the home He left in order to come to earth—His Heavenly home. From all eternity His dwelling place had been filled with unimaginable glory and splendor. And yet, the Bible says, He "emptied himself . . . being born in human likeness" (Philippians 2:7 NRSV). Out of love for you and me, He left Heaven's glory for earth's misery.

But the story doesn't end there. Now He has returned to Heaven—and someday we will join Him. Think of it. He wants to share Heaven's glory with us! One evening a little girl was taking a walk with her father. Looking up at the stars she exclaimed, "Daddy, if the wrong side of heaven is so beautiful, what must the right side be like!"

UNLOAD YOUR DISTRESS

[Cast] all your care upon Him, for He cares for you.

1 PETER 5:7

I've been told that the French translation of this phrase, "Cast all your care upon Him" is "Unload your distresses upon God." Have you ever seen a dump truck get rid of its load? The driver simply pushes a button or pulls on a lever and the heavy load is discharged at the prescribed spot. The truck would be of no use if it carried its burden forever.

We were never meant to be crushed under the weight of care. We can push the button of faith or pull the lever of trust, and our burden is discharged upon the shoulder of Him who said He would gladly bear it. Unload the anxieties of the present moment upon Him, for He cares for you. If He loved you enough to take away the burden of your sins, can't you trust Him to take away every lesser burden as well?

THREE IN ONE

Every spirit that confesses that Jesus Christ has come in the flesh is of God.

1 JOHN 4:2

The Bible clearly teaches that God comes to us in three distinct ways: as Father, Son, and Holy Spirit. At the end of one of his letters, Paul wrote, "May the grace of the Lord Jesus Christ, and the love of God, and the fellowship of the Holy Spirit be with you all" (2 Corinthians 13:14 NIV). All three are distinct, and yet they are also united as one. We worship one God, who reveals Himself to us in three persons.

How can we visualize this? When St. Patrick first brought Christianity to Ireland, it is said that he used a clover leaf to explain the Trinity to new converts: three separate leaves, and yet combined in only one plant. Water can be a solid, or a liquid, or a gas—but it is all water. Sometimes when I go into a church I notice trefoil windows—windows in the form of three interlocking circles. Each circle is separate, and yet together they form a single design, symbolizing the Trinity. A mystery? Yes—but also a source of great comfort.

A Victorious Christian

The Spirit also helps in our weaknesses.

ROMANS 8:26

We need to rely constantly on the Holy Spirit. We need to remember that Christ dwells in us through the Holy Spirit. Our bodies are the dwelling place of the Third Person of the Trinity. Why don't we rely on Him as we should? We don't realize how weak we are. We don't realize how strong our enemy is. We may even doubt if God is really going to help us. Or we think we can do it all ourselves—or that we must. But we should ask Him to do it all and to take over in our lives. We should tell Him how weak, helpless, unstable, and unreliable we are. It is important that we stand aside and let Him take over in all our choices and decisions. We know that the Holy Spirit prays for us (Romans 8:26), and what a comfort that should be to the weakest of us.

A victorious Christian is one who, in spite of worries, inner conflicts, and tensions, is confident that God is in control and will be victorious in the end. Whatever our difficulties, whatever our circumstances, we must remember, as Corrie ten Boom used to say, "Jesus is victor!"

A Glorious Promise!

*"I am the resurrection and the life. He who believes in
Me, though he may die, he shall live."*

John 11:25

In Heaven we will be like Christ. Someday God's plan to
make us more like Christ will be complete, for "we will all
be changed—in a flash, in the twinkling of an eye, at the
last trumpet" (1 Corinthians 15:51–52 NIV).

What does this mean? First, it means we will have new
bodies—bodies that will be like Christ's resurrection
body. Do I know what we'll look like in Heaven? No—
but our new bodies will be perfect, beyond the reach of
all illness and decay. It also means our whole nature will
be transformed. Someday we will be like Christ! Now we
love imperfectly—but not then. Now our joy and peace
are tempered by sorrow and turmoil—but not then. The
Bible says, "Dear friends, now we are children of God,
and what we will be has not yet been made known. But
we know that when Christ appears, we shall be like him,
for we shall see him as he is" (1 John 3:2 NIV). What a
glorious promise!

It Was Love

"I have loved you with an everlasting love; therefore with lovingkindness I have drawn you."

JEREMIAH 31:3

Many people have difficulty believing God is a God of love. "How could He be," they ask, "when the world is filled with so much suffering and evil?" It is not an easy issue—but if you really want to know the reality of God's love, look at the Cross. It was love, divine love, that made Christ endure the Cross, despising the shame. It was love that restrained Him when He was falsely accused of blasphemy and led to Golgotha to die with common thieves. He raised not a hand against His enemies. It was love that kept Him from calling legions of angels to come to His defense. It was love that made Him, in a moment of agonizing pain, pause and give hope to a repentant sinner who cried, "Lord, remember me when You come into Your kingdom" (Luke 23:42).

It was love that caused Jesus to lift His voice and pray, "Father, forgive them, for they do not know what they do" (Luke 23:34). Does God love us? Yes—and the proof is the Cross.

HEAVEN IS REAL

We, according to His promise, look for new heavens and a new earth in which righteousness dwells.

2 PETER 3:13

"Life is hard—but God is good and Heaven is real." This is what a doctor friend of mine sometimes tells his Christian patients because he knows how easily we get caught up in our present problems and forget God's promise of Heaven. Paul wrote, "If only for this life we have hope in Christ, we are of all people most to be pitied" (1 Corinthians 15:19 NIV). But our hope isn't only for this life! In the midst of life's storms, our hope in God's promise of Heaven is "an anchor for the soul, firm and secure" (Hebrews 6:19 NIV).

When we know Christ, we know life isn't meaningless, because God has a reason for keeping us here. Every day is a gift from Him and is another opportunity to love Him and serve Him. Heaven doesn't make this life less important; it makes it more important.

Not Faith but Sight

"The Son of Man will come in the glory of His Father with His angels."

MATTHEW 16:27

Today Christ is hidden from our view (although through the Holy Spirit He lives in our hearts). Today is the day of faith; as Paul wrote, "We walk by faith, not by sight" (2 Corinthians 5:7). Only in the future will we "see Him as He is" (1 John 3:2).

Christ's first appearing was quiet, almost unnoticed—a humble manger, simple shepherds, an insignificant corner of the Roman Empire. His second appearing will be glorious and universal. He will be accompanied by His angels and will defeat every enemy until He subdues the whole earth.

How easily the events of the moment crowd out the promise of eternity! The present seems so real; the unseen future seems so illusory. But in reality the opposite is true. Don't let the present consume you. Instead, "seek those things which are above, where Christ is" (Colossians 3:1).

OUR SURE HOPE

*The Lord will deliver me from every evil work and
preserve me for His heavenly kingdom.*

2 TIMOTHY 4:18

Why did Jesus Christ leave Heaven's glory and enter this sin-infested world? For one reason: to make our eternal salvation possible. When God created Adam and Eve, His plan was that they would live in perfect harmony with Him forever.

But Satan was determined to change that, and with his lies, he lured them away from God. When that happened, death came upon the human race, and we are all its victims. Never forget: death was Satan's greatest victory.

But by His death and resurrection Jesus Christ reversed this. Satan's greatest victory has now been turned into defeat! Death has now been put to death! No wonder the Bible says, "'Where, O death, is your victory? Where, O death, is your sting?' . . . Thanks be to God! He gives us the victory through our Lord Jesus Christ" (1 Corinthians 15:55, 57 NIV).

Christ's motive in coming to earth was love, and His goal was to destroy death and take us to be with the Father forever. This is our sure hope.

Resting Faith

The testing of your faith produces patience.

James 1:3

Dwight L. Moody was fond of pointing out that there are three kinds of faith in Jesus Christ: struggling faith, which is like a man floundering and fearful in deep water; clinging faith, which is like a man hanging to the side of a boat; and resting faith, which is like a man safe inside the boat—strong and secure enough to reach out his hand to help someone else.

Notice each man had faith. Each knew the boat was his only hope. But only one had a resting faith. Only one had discovered he could actually be in the boat—where all he had to do was rest. This is the kind of faith God wants us to have—a faith that trusts Him totally. But sometimes we discover its reality only after we have endured a struggling or clinging faith. Sometimes we only realize we can get in the boat when the storm rages and we cry out to God with new faith. Then our Savior graciously extends His hand and says, "Come to Me . . . and I will give you rest" (Matthew 11:28).

PRAY WITHOUT CEASING

Men always ought to pray and not lose heart.

LUKE 18:1

A prayer does not have to be eloquent or contain the language and terms of a theologian. In fact, sometimes our simplest, most heartfelt prayers are the most pleasing to God.

When you made your decision for Christ, you became a child of God, adopted by Him into His family forever. Now you have the wonderful privilege of coming directly into His presence and addressing God as your Father. In the beginning you may not be fluent, but it's important to begin. My wife has a notebook she has kept of our children as they were beginning to talk. She treasures these first attempts, mistakes and all. She said, "I wouldn't take anything for that book."

When Paul said we should "pray without ceasing" (1 Thessalonians 5:17) he chose a term used in his day to describe a persistent cough. Repeatedly, throughout our day, we should be turning quickly to God to praise and thank Him, and to ask for His help. God is interested in everything we do, and nothing is too great or too insignificant to share with Him.

With God Forever!

We are . . . pleased rather to be absent from the body and to be present with the Lord.

2 Corinthians 5:8

Heaven is many things, but the most important is this: Heaven is God's dwelling place. It is the place where God lives! It's true that God is everywhere, but Heaven is more than a place; it is a whole different dimension of existence, and God is in its midst, with Christ at His right hand. The Bible says, "we will be with the Lord forever" (1 Thessalonians 4:17 NIV).

Think of it: we will be with God forever! And because we will be with Him, we will be absolutely safe from all evil. Sorrow and suffering will never again touch us—never. One of the most moving passages in all the Bible is found in its next to last chapter: "And I heard a loud voice from the throne saying, 'Look! God's dwelling place is now among the people, and he will dwell with them. They will be his people, and God himself will be with them and be their God. He will wipe every tear from their eyes. There will be no more death or mourning or crying or pain, for the old order of things has passed away'" (Revelation 21:3–4 NIV). Praise God for the hope we have in Christ!

NOTES

NOTES

NOTES

NOTES